I0483122

Six Sigma Marketing

By Ade Asefeso MCIPS MBA

Second Edition

ISBN-13: 978-1499542080

ISBN-10: 1499542089

Publisher: AA Global Sourcing Ltd
Website: http://www.aaglobalsourcing.com

Table of Contents

Disclaimer

This publication is designed to provide competent and reliable information regarding the subject matter covered. However, it is sold with the understanding that the author and publisher are not engaged in rendering professional advice. The authors and publishers specifically disclaim any liability that is incurred from the use or application of contents of this book.

If you purchased this book without a cover you should be aware that this book may have been stolen property and reported as "unsold and destroyed" to the publisher. In this case neither the author nor the publisher has received any payment for this "stripped book."

Dedication

To my family and friends who seems to have been sent here to teach me something about who I am supposed to be. They have nurtured me, challenged me, and even opposed me.... But at every juncture has taught me!

This book is dedicated to my lovely boys, Thomas, Michael and Karl. Teaching them to manage their finance will give them the lives they deserve. They have taught me more about life, presence, and energy management than anything I have done in my life.

Chapter 1: Introduction

Many Sales and Marketing managers may be unfamiliar with Six Sigma and why it is important in Sales and Marketing. Here is a brief introduction to its terms and how it might apply in our world. Six Sigma is a disciplined methodology that uses data and statistical analysis to measure and improve a company's operational performance. It focuses on identifying and eliminating "defects" in business processes and has produced hundreds of millions of dollars in new profitability in a wide variety of industries.

Why should Sales and Marketing care about Six Sigma?

Six Sigma professionals and Sales and Marketing professionals have similar objectives in mind; finding the path of least resistance and sticking to what works best. The difference is that Sales and Marketing often rely on intuition and judgment, while Six Sigma relies strictly on scientific analysis of data (facts, figures). The Six Sigma Methodology is responsible for billions of dollars in profit improvements in hundreds of companies. Although its origins are in manufacturing, it has also been effective in finance and service industries (called transactional industries) and in fields as diverse as healthcare and software development. Now, attention is turning to how Six Sigma can help Sales and Marketing organizations as well. It has been tried already, to be sure, with successes and some failures unfolding as we speak, just like at the beginning of any new idea.

What does the term "Six Sigma" mean?

"Sigma" is a statistical term for the measures of variability.

- "One" Sigma is a very high degree of variability (Seven "mistakes" out of ten opportunities)
- "Six" Sigma is a very low degree of variability (3.4 "mistakes" out of 1,000,000 opportunities)

If you have a close ratio of 30%, your sales process can be said to be operating at one sigma!

What is the Six Sigma Methodology?

Six Sigma's magic doesn't lie in statistical or high-tech razzle dazzle. Six Sigma relies on tried-and-true methods that have been around for decades. In fact, Six Sigma discards a great deal of the complexity that characterizes total quality management (TQM).

The Six Sigma Methodology

Define improvement activity goals. At the top level these can be the organization's strategic objectives, such as return on investment or market share. At the project level, they might be reducing defects or increasing yield.

Measure the existing system. Establish valid and reasonable metrics to help you monitor progress toward the goals.

Analyze the system. Identify ways to eliminate the gap between current and desired performance. Apply statistical tools to guide the analysis.

Improve the system. Be creative in finding new ways to do things safer, better, cheaper, or faster. Use project management techniques to implement the changes. Use statistical methods to validate the improvements.
Control the new system. Institutionalize the new system by modifying compensation and incentives, policies, procedures, budgets and other management systems.

How does Six Sigma Work?

The Six Sigma approach attempts to translate cause and effect into a mathematical expression. The form of that expression is $Y = f(x)$. It is a way of defining the relationship between independent variables (x) and dependent variables (Y), where "f" stands for the relationship (in mathematical terms).

How is Six Sigma deployed in a company?

The primary means of deploying Six Sigma (especially in large companies) is to establish an infrastructure of people trained in the methodology and accountable for implementing it to produce results. "Black Belts" and "Master Black Belts" work full time on projects and are the most knowledgeable in the approach. "Green Belts" spend some time working on projects while maintaining their regular work responsibilities. "Process Owners" are traditional line managers whose operations are the focus of Six Sigma projects.

How does Six Sigma apply in marketing and sales?

Six Sigma can apply to any goal-directed work activity of an organization. The pre-requisite is the work needs to be well-organized and defined (objectives, activities, measurements).

The first step of Six Sigma (Define) attempts to ensure this. In marketing, in sales, it means defining the basic value proposition, market segmentation, and work flow necessary for measurements to be meaningful and reliable. Often, this improvement alone improves results. After the basics are in place, the statistical power of Six Sigma can be applied in depth.

Chapter 2: The History of Six Sigma

Since its introduction at Motorola in the late 1980s, Six Sigma has assumed multiple aliases; operations excellence, business process improvement and process excellence. Regardless of the moniker used, the goal of Six Sigma companies has remained consistent; to encourage continuous process improvement by using a standardized, documented and repeatable problem solving methodology.

Six Sigma provides a common language and method to address business opportunities and solve business problems. It also provides a roadmap that shows problem solvers where to start and what to do next. Although common tools and language are used, Six Sigma is flexible enough to be applied to different challenges throughout business, wherever they might arise either in manufacturing, finance, procurement, sales, marketing or any other functional area.

Since the early days of Six Sigma, there has been an unfortunate but common perception that Six Sigma can improve only pure manufacturing processes and that a fact based problem solving methodology does not transfer well to transactional processes, specifically sales and marketing.

Most of the nonbelievers question the ability and effectiveness of applying a standardized problem solving method to the art of sales and marketing.

They believe theirs is such a dynamic and sometimes nebulous environment that a structured approach requiring processes metrics and data.

Six Sigma does not suppress creativity; rather, it provides a framework to channel it. Six Sigma provides practical guidance on how to begin the process of solving a problem and supplies questions to ask along the way. Creativity flourishes in the content and throughput of a successful solution, not in the tools used to achieve the outcome. Six Sigma is the engine that drives results; creativity is the fuel. Although Six Sigma has been very popular in manufacturing for over a decade, sales and marketing leaders have only recently started to use it.

This delayed appreciation is the result of four main factors:

1. Facilities: In most manufacturing processes, almost every variable can be precisely controlled. Reducing defects and improving efficiency is already ingrained in the psyche and culture. Manufacturing facilities provide fertile soil for the application of problem solving methods that focus on measuring processes and tightly controlling input variables to achieve optimal outcomes. Forerunners of Six Sigma, such as statistical process control (SPC), total quality management (TQM) and ISO 9000 methodologies, attest to this mindset and have been used for years in manufacturing settings.

2. Professional backgrounds: For years, the majority of Six Sigma professionals hailed from

12

manufacturing. These individuals are often less familiar with transactional processes and might not recognize the potential for applying Six Sigma there. This lack of understanding is significant, because to successfully apply Six Sigma one must be familiar with both the Six Sigma tools and the environment in which they are being applied. After all, an auto mechanic would certainly feel more comfortable using a new set of pliers in a garage than in an operating room, even though the tool is appropriate in both environments.

3. Consumer purchasing patterns: For a company to dedicate itself to any improvement effort there must be a strong cause for action. Manufacturing had that cause for action. The globalization of the world economy removed barriers of entry for low cost manufacturers into established markets. These new, low cost, high quality competitors forced traditional manufacturers to search for opportunities to improve their operations. The result of this increased competition was a commensurate increase in the supply of most products at reduced prices.

Improved manufacturing techniques and increases in sales drove record revenues that masked any need for improved sales and marketing efficiencies. Fat bottom lines led many sales and marketing professionals to ask, "Why should we worry about process improvements while sales and revenue are increasing at record levels?" This attitude, though logically achieved, prevented the arrival of the required cause for action in sales and marketing. Interestingly, this same thinking originally delayed structured process improvements in many manufacturing environments.

4. Existing sales culture: Sales' entrepreneurial spirit actively resists standardized processes and encourages independence. If Six Sigma is misconstrued as negatively impacting this spirit, it will be opposed. Applying Six Sigma requires altering both processes and attitudes. When everything seems to be working well, it is difficult to convince people change is needed. Only recently have many CEOs started to investigate the potential for trying to apply Six Sigma to non-manufacturing processes.

Evolution of Six Sigma

Six Sigma has evolved from shop floor applications of Statistical process control (SPC) to the current state of applying processes and measures to all business processes. This progression can be perceived as advancing through three main stages, with the third stage currently underway.

Manufacturing stage: The genesis of Six Sigma and still the most fertile soil in terms of ease of application is in manufacturing. Manufacturing facilities are usually led by engineers who are familiar with the define, measure, analyze, improve and control concept; whether they have been formally trained or not. There is little need to convince them of the advantage of tracking defects back to their sources, trying to identify the root causes of failure and then implementing a controlled solution.

Finance and information management stage: As business leaders became aware of the improvements Six Sigma was driving in manufacturing, they rushed to apply it to other business functions in hopes of reaping similar benefits. The next logical place was in data rich environments that mirror manufacturing's need for repeatable processes and minimal defects. This led to Six Sigma's introduction into finance and information management. A finance department requires a robust and defect free process to effectively close the books, pay royalties, track expenses, and pay salaries and commissions. The recently introduced Sarbanes-Oxley regulations mandate documented repeatable financial processes. The opportunities to optimize these processes have resulted in the recent embrace of Six Sigma by financial service companies including Bank of America, Merrill Lynch and American Express. Imagine the money and effort that could be saved if finance departments could accurately close a quarter in a few days vs. two weeks.

Information management also needs robust processes to efficiently and effectively provide software, deliver hardware and manage data. Six Sigma provides tools to help accomplish these tasks. Finance and information management are usually led and staffed by individuals who recognize and appreciate the advantages of standardized processes. Six Sigma has fulfilled this need for structure in both functions. The first two stages in the evolution of Six Sigma from manufacturing to finance and information management are well established.

Transactional process stage: The third, and ongoing, stage in the evolution of Six Sigma is its application to transactional processes, most notably in sales and marketing. This has proven to be the most difficult stage in the growth of Six Sigma as a cross-functional application. Some of the reasons for this challenge are the difficulty of identifying appropriate projects and driving the culture shift required for transactional leaders to embrace the concept. Driving this change is difficult but worth pursuing. Significant savings can be realized from improved transactional processes because, unlike most manufacturing efficiency gains, improved sales processes directly impact top-line sales and therefore bottom-line profit. Unfortunately, a lack of precise control over many of the variables in transactional processes has restricted the use of Six Sigma. There is an approximate inverse relationship between the ease of application of Six Sigma and potential savings it can drive. Unlike in manufacturing, the most important and least controllable variable in transactional processes is the human element. In a manufacturing process, many of the process steps are automated and, once set, free of excessive human interference. Because these steps usually can be precisely adjusted and controlled, it is not unusual to achieve very high correlations between the quality of process inputs and the quality of process outputs.

Human activities, on the other hand, are far less controllable or predictable. Therefore, processes that require high human input eschew control. The linkages between inputs and outputs are simply not as easy to adjust as they are in manufacturing processes.

16

Additionally, in sales and marketing processes variables such as customers, competitors and the weather are completely uncontrollable but have a huge impact on process outcomes. These challenges should not be construed as reason to abandon the idea that Six Sigma can work in this environment, but the reality is that fewer process variables are controllable. Six Sigma should simply be applied to those variables that can be controlled. This might not lead to the near perfect correlations that are seen in manufacturing projects, but correlations of more than 50 to 60% can still be achieved. They provide strong directional accuracy not available prior to the implementation of Six Sigma. In a world where 20% margins and 10% growth are considered success, making critical decisions with 50 to 60% certainty, rather than 0%, is an enormous and profitable improvement.

Chapter 3: Myth that Six Sigma is Only for Operations

To convert the critics who question the applicability of Six Sigma in the transactional arena, the root of their cynicism can often be identified through a few easy questions.

1. Why don't you believe it will work?
2. Do you think there is not enough data in a transactional environment for Six Sigma to work?
3. Are your sales or marketing processes so strong they cannot be improved?
4. Are you concerned the people who work in these areas do not have the intellectual bandwidth, desire or willingness to deal with the slight amount of math that some Six Sigma projects require?

The answers to these questions generally expose prejudices about the value of Six Sigma and how it is applied, but they rarely reveal fact based reasons for rejection. At its core, Six Sigma is all about finding the root cause of a problem and solving it. The same approach should be applied to finding the root cause of scepticism toward applying it to transactional processes. Efficient sales and marketing processes are critically important to business; a defined approach to solving problems that can pay remarkable dividends.

Sales and marketing are closer to customers than any other business functions and generate the fuel on which businesses run cash. Meeting customers' desires should be a company's single most important task. Meeting customer desires should drive the overall strategy of every business. Ultimately, it should determine what a company makes and sells.

The transactional environment is filled with data on sales, markets, territories, sales representatives and customers. Sales and marketing professionals are constantly pursuing market data and competitive intelligence to determine how well they are fulfilling their customers' unmet needs, how well they are penetrating new environments, and the impact of newly launched products on sales, revenue, customers, and competitors. Six Sigma provides the roadmap to capture this data, analyze it and foster decisions based on it.

Having a customer choose to pay for your product or service over a competitor's is the ultimate goal of any sales or marketing organization. This purchase is the ultimate throughput of multiple process steps, some controllable and some not. Even a slight improvement in the effectiveness of a few of these controllable process steps will lead to the improved throughput of the process. A generic sales process includes:

- Prospecting customers.
- Building rapport.
- Identifying needs.
- Presenting solution(s).
- Overcoming objections.
- Closing the sale.

The ultimate effectiveness of the process is calculated by multiplying the effectiveness of each step. This calculation is called a rolled throughput yield (RTY). The RTY is analogous to the efficiency of a bucket brigade; a chain of people working to put out a fire by passing buckets of water from person to person. Imagine there are five people in the chain and each one spills 10% of the water from the bucket as he or she passes it to the next person. In other words, each person is 90% efficient at transporting the water. At the end of the chain, the bucket will have lost quite a bit of water. The efficiency of the bucket brigade is calculated by multiplying the efficiencies of each member of the team. 0.90 X 0.90 X 0.90 X 0.90 X 0.90 = 0.591. Even though each individual is 90% effective, the team is collectively only 59% efficient; 41% of the water is wasted.

The RTY of the sales process can be similarly calculated. The RTY also shows how a large overall process improvement can be driven by only slight improvements to individual process steps. If a sales representative is 90% efficient at each step in the sales process, at the end of the process the sales representative will be successful 59% of the time. If the sales rep is able to improve his or her efficiency by only 5% per process step, to 95%, the RTY of the process will improve to; 0.95 X 0.95 X 0.95 X 0.95 X 0.95 = 0.774. Just a slight improvement to each step in the sales process has improved sales from 59 to 77%, an improvement of 18%. If a sales process were previously generating $1 million, this level of improvement would result in an additional $180,000.

If common, end-to-end process steps are closely observed, documented and studied, and if the data they produce are collected and analyzed, it is possible to identify improvement opportunities within the process. The newly refined process can become a competitive advantage. Once the science of the sales process is identified and documented, more effort can be applied to refining the art of the sale.

There are multiple opportunities to improve sales and marketing processes. Clearly, selling a product to a customer is the most important process in sales and marketing. This is an obvious area to focus Six Sigma efforts, but not the only area. Additional sales processes that could make use of Six Sigma include.

- Interviewing and hiring successful sales representatives.
- Training sales representatives on both the sales process and the various products and services about which they are expected to be experts.
- Defining the most efficient way to manage a sales representative's samples stock.
- Identifying and nurturing the most profitable customers and territories.
- Moving marketing materials through copy review.

These are common processes that both sales and marketing groups need to focus on in order to be successful. None require the magic of relationship building or personal charisma; they just require rigor.

Some have insinuated that one reason salespeople avoid Six Sigma is because it is too hard. To suggest sales and marketing professionals can't handle the Six

Sigma methodology or the math skills it may require simply does not reflect the profile of successful salespeople. The financial rewards from a successful sales career are significantly higher than most other professions.

The fruits of a successful sales career create competition for those roles. In a competitive market, sales professionals cannot achieve success without strong intellectual capacity. These financial rewards inspire many of the best and the brightest to pursue careers in business, as opposed to law, medicine or science. Successful sales professionals can maintain this lead throughout their careers.

The perceived complexity of Six Sigma is not the reason it has not been successful in sales and marketing. The reason is an unwillingness of sales and marketing leadership to embrace the methodology. The people involved in transactional processes are often unwilling to adopt a measurement based methodology in a business function they see as being driven purely by relationships and the strength of their personalities. Adopting Six Sigma represents change, and people do not like change, especially change that seems counterintuitive to what has worked for them in the past.

There might be a concern that the attributes and capabilities that have fuelled past success relationship building, creativity and market knowledge will not be useful in a Six Sigma environment. Salespeople might fear that a lack of math acumen will be exposed during Six Sigma training. These fears are common, but unfounded.

Those who are able to navigate a successful sales career are equally capable of not only handling but also mastering Six Sigma, regardless of what they studied in college. It is also worth mentioning that very little statistics or math is actually required to employ Six Sigma. Many of the most useful Six Sigma tools such as a process map or a prioritization matrix are simple. Both of these tools can drive significant process improvement and do not require any statistics. The statistical tools that Six Sigma uses are basic and have been successfully taught to millions of non-statisticians and math phobics. Even though there are plenty of very complex statistical tools, the simple ones usually provide sufficient answers.

A carpenter certainly can produce great results with laser guides, pneumatic nail guns and electric compound mitre saws, but he can also achieve great results with a hammer, screwdriver and pair of vise grips. The judicious use of simple tools can produce great results.

Chapter 4: Six Sigma Marketing Strategy

As we say at AA Global Sourcing, know-how is only 20% of the equation. Know-why is 80%. Or is it 90%...? Whatever. We will let you argue the numbers. But this much is certainly true; if you are not asking why you are doing things, then you are severely limiting the impact of how you are doing things.

Let's take this a step beyond the surface.

Tell me, what do a top surgeon and an annoying five-year old have in common? Answer: they ask "why?" And if they are not getting the answers they are looking for, then I will bet you a cup of coffee that they keep asking "why" until they do.

Can you say "why?" Good. This chapter is for you.

Six Sigma principles prescribe a set of standards to improve performance, create efficiencies and decrease defects. Though popularized in the operations functions of numerous companies, Six Sigma principles are effective through all functions, including marketing. Let's apply the five phases of Six Sigma methodology to your own business case.

Define

Define the goal(s) of your strategic marketing plan. What's most relevant? Is it to gather business intelligence? Develop pricing models? Counter low-cost rivals? Reposition the business? Whatever it is, it must be specific and root-oriented (i.e. tied to your most important business problem).

Measure

What must be measured to track progress towards the determined goal? A few examples might be (a) profitability, (b) customer lifetime value, (c) conversion rate, and/or (d) number of business leads. Ideally, make the key performance metric you are tracking long-term focused. Otherwise, you will fall into a common pitfall which is that your marketing strategy will be more tactical than strategic.

Analyze

This step translates the key performance metric into key insights that can be relayed into actionable intelligence. In other words, this step makes the data meaningful. The process for analysis must be collaborative across all functions to ensure objectivity and productivity. We recommend bringing in key members from each business function or business unit to participate is seeing what the numbers mean.

Improve

After deciphering the meaning of the data, the same group should devise scenarios to test that will theoretically improve the data going forward. The benefit here is that the organization will feel 'smaller' with more speed in decision making and agility in business manoeuvres. The result marketing tests should be systematic, with the aim of improving metric performance. For instance, if you have a goal to counter low-cost rivals by increasing customer lifetime value (CLV), then you might experiment with blogging or sequential email sends to improve CLV.

Control

You did think this is self-explanatory but this is undoubtedly the most overlooked phase. Perhaps most professionals figure that the tests are so bullet-proof that they give control only a cursory scan. Regardless, you must get this phase right. Assign leading and lagging indicators to the tests to track progress. This will mitigate risk of failed tests and instil the imperative of maintaining long-term discipline.

The beauty of Six Sigma and its principles is that it imposes the sequence that why must come before how, what, and where. It's as fail-safe a way of instituting a culture of strategy before tactics.

Chapter 5: Six Sigma for Marketing Processes

Six Sigma for Sales and Marketing is relatively new approach to enable and sustain growth. They are part of the bright future offered by adapting Six Sigma to the growth arena. The linkage of Six Sigma for Marketing and Six Sigma for Sales tasks and tools to strategic, tactical, and operational processes is where the Six Sigma discipline adds measurable value to Sales and Marketing team performance.

Imagine the possibilities if you possessed a crystal ball that let you predict the future. You would know what will work and what won't work to create and sustain growth. You would know when to correct for competitive and environmental changes and how to prevent going off-course. Is this a fantasy? Can a business predict (with some certainty) what will drive success and how to stay on the right track? We believe the answer is yes. The appropriate data can inform executives, with high probability, whether the critical elements of the business are performing as planned to achieve desired results.

Performance against plan is how a business typically defines success. Businesses gauge success by a multitude of metrics; revenue, income, profit, customer satisfaction, market share, return on equity, return on assets, return on investments, and so on. Bottom-line, planned success means reaching and sustaining goals over time usually growth goals. The challenge lies in determining the vital few results to focus on and the critical metrics that best monitor performance. The Fortune 500 list serves as another metric of success. Of the top 100 companies, 70 have been in the top 100 for five or more years. Interestingly, 63% of those 70 companies acknowledge implementing Six Sigma to some degree. Through further analysis, we have found that these same 44 Six Sigma users also reported on average 49% higher profits (compounded annually) and 2% higher Compounded Annual Growth Revenue (CAGR) than their peers. Notice how the profits outpaced the revenue growth for this group of companies. More than likely, they employ the "traditional" Six Sigma cost-cutting approach. Imagine the benefit these firms will enjoy when they also begin to apply Six Sigma to the top line to drive revenue. If they deploy Six Sigma into Sales and Marketing with as much discipline and rigor as they did to eliminate waste in manufacturing and engineering, these firms' CAGR will outrun their competitors as much as their profits have, and they will easily secure a prominent spot on the Top 100 list for another five or more years.

Benchmarking tells us that successful companies, which effectively implement Six Sigma tools, methods, and best practices, find the following benefits.

- **Systematic innovation:** Generate and define more ideas linked with market opportunities in a structured way.
- **Manage risk better:** Identify critical issues early in the commercialization process such

that plans can be developed to mitigate or eliminate risk going forward.

- **Higher return yield from a project portfolio:** Avoid overloading resources with too many low-risks, small-gain projects through a discriminating selection process.

Select fewer projects: The "best fit" projects, not necessarily the easiest projects. Business leaders often hold Sales and Marketing accountable for driving revenue growth; the panacea for most business ills. They want these teams to improve their accuracy rate of committing to, and achieving, their goals. Marketing executives seek new ideas to bolster their success rate. Applying Six Sigma to marketing may be a new approach, but it comes with an "insurance policy." Six Sigma has a proven track record in other parts of the business. Six Sigma concepts can provide additive elements to increase the competitive advantage marketing needs to act proactively, sustain its positive momentum, and keep pace with the ever-changing landscape.

To tailor Six Sigma to marketing, you start with an overview of how it works. We find that marketing professionals rarely view their own work as process-oriented; it often is depicted as project or activity-based. However, the American Marketing Association (AMA) defines "marketing" as "a set of processes for creating, communicating, and delivering value to customers and managing customer relationships in ways that benefit the organization and stakeholders." The American Heritage Dictionary describes a "process" as a "series of actions, changes, or functions bringing about a result" and a "function" as "something closely related to another thing and dependent on it for its existence, value, or significance." Others define "marketing" as the process to identify, anticipate, and then meet customers' needs and requirements. This definition seems narrow. In a special issue of Journal of Marketing (1999, Volume 63, pp. 180–197), Christine Moorman and Roland Rust propose that the marketing function should play a key role in managing several important connections between the customer and critical firm elements, including connecting the customer to (1) the product, (2) service delivery, and (3) financial accountability. Marketing's value is found to be a function of the degree to which it develops knowledge and skills in connecting the customer to the product and to financial accountability.

Hence, to fully capture marketing's value, the customization of Six Sigma should span the scope of connecting the customer to the product and to financial accountability.

Moorman and Rust's research suggests that the value of the marketing function is due to how well-developed the methodologies are for facilitating the customer-product connection. Marketing's customer-financial accountability linkage often is not well understood, but it needs to account for profitability considerations in attracting and retaining customers. It is not about cost; it is about profitable growth. Ideally, marketing should effectively and efficiently create and sustain growth for the firm. How is that best done? A challenge is to determine which marketing methodology best facilitates the customer-product-financial linkages. The marketing methodology should nurture and channel the firm's important creativity and growth capabilities.

Chapter 6: Six Sigma and its Use in Marketing

The Six Sigma discipline gives business leaders the opportunity to drive more fact-based decisions into managing the business. Six Sigma has been successfully applied to the technical aspects of a business (such as engineering and manufacturing). A new effort is afoot to bring Six Sigma into the "softer" side of business, marketing. By adding more "science" to the "art" of marketing, the Six Sigma approach can be the next best thing to a crystal ball!

A decision-making process that lacks the appropriate facts causes leaders to fill the void with intuition. If facts are absent, statistically grounded probabilities can strengthen decision-making. Marketing executives should shed their use of intuition (or "gut feeling") to solve business issues and/or drive growth. Columnist and author Marilyn Savant said, "Not knowing the difference between opinion and fact makes it difficult to make decisions". Intuition sneaks into every business at some point. The objective is to recognize it when it appears and to deal with it directly by using facts to support or deny the "hypothesis." Bernard Baruch, an advisor to six U.S. presidents, said, "Every man has the right to be wrong in his opinions. But no man has a right to be wrong about his facts".

The Six Sigma concept has evolved over the past several decades to represent a set of fundamental business concepts that puts customers first and uses fact-based decision-making to drive improvements. It was first used in the U.S. at Motorola to cut costs by reducing variation in manufacturing. This book represents the next evolution of Six Sigma; a marketing application. We believe a unique view of Six Sigma's techniques and tools can be applied to drive income growth. It is our experience that companies are only beginning to implement Six Sigma to drive sales and marketing; however, the idea is increasingly discussed. In the fall of 2005, the Worldwide Conventions and Business Forums (WCBF) held its second annual conference on Six Sigma in sales and marketing. This is a cutting-edge application of Six Sigma.

Six Sigma has recently moved from being solely meant for manufacturing processes to front office procedures. This is often referred to as Business Process Improvement or shortened as BPI and is a new concept in the business industry. This migration has potential to improve businesses in many other aspects of work. This is especially effective where many businesses are experiencing a decrease in margins and an increase in marketing costs. Business Process Improvement within this methodology is capable of improving both margin and revenue successfully over time.

Both BPI and its correlation with Six Sigma is not a necessarily new concept, but it has been recently acknowledged as an effective one. Many direct marketers are already familiar with the concept especially when trying to improve campaigns and measure its effects on the current market. At first, these concepts may seem rather confusing and complicated but can be likened to amending the instructions on a shampoo bottle. Instead of saying: "wash, rinse and repeat" a Six Sigma amendment may state "wash twice and on the second wash do it more vigorously".

Using this process in the marketing phase of business employs some very useful tools like process maps, fishbone diagrams, pareto charts, and brainstorming. There are also other very effective tools such as the Design of Experiments with the use of Full Factorials.

These tools are very useful but are not the most important processes needed to fully implement Six Sigma in marketing. It is mostly summed up as understanding the processes within marketing and executing improvements within these processes continuously over time. This will successfully produce several measured and desired results.

There are four main principles when implementing BPI or Six Sigma in marketing.

- The first has to do with realizing that there are 3 main sources of revenue within a company. These sources of revenue are acquired through adding new customers, getting old or existing customers to buy more, and getting these customers to buy more frequently.
- Secondly, identifying the process is needed in order to bring about the 3 sources above. This is essentially a choice between creating a new process or working on improving one that already exists.

- Third, breaking down the process is the next step to successfully integrating these methodologies into the marketing realm of business. This can be done by identifying all the variables within the process. In the business of marketing this is usually subjective but in some cases these variables can be quantified.
- Lastly, use procedures such as the DMAIC framework to help control or improve the initial process. If this process is followed, any company will have successfully sorted and solved an issue or achieved a new goal in their marketing campaign.

Central themes of Six Sigma.

Focus on the customer: Understanding your customer and his buying process can lead to monumental improvements. Centre your marketing on what drives customer satisfaction and value.

Focus on processes rather than the end result: By analyzing and fixing the process itself, companies will build competitive advantage over their competition.

Collaboration: If all parts of the organization including strategic partners and vendors need to keep their focus on the customer. Improving teamwork between all parts of the organization especially breaking down barriers between sales and marketing is essential.

Defining goals and setting clear priorities with frequent reviews: Allow you to focus on correcting the process rather than "putting out fires."

Continuous Improvement: This will push your organization to higher and higher levels. It will become your strategic advantage over your competition.

Six sigma is such a good fit for the marketing process that you wonder why it was not developed for that part of the business first.

Chapter 7: Six Sigma's Application Argument

There is a battle being waged on the fringe of the Six Sigma community. The battle is over how to apply Six Sigma to one of the last frontiers of business – marketing. There are two sides to the argument; those who favour a direct application, and those who feel the method should be modified. While the first approach may lead to less costly practices, the latter cannot only make a marketing department more efficient, but also more effective.

The Direct Application Argument

On one side of the Six Sigma and marketing argument are those who feel that Six Sigma and its tools should be applied on a project by project basis to such marketing activities as sales, promotion and distribution. Extending the cost cutting focus of Six Sigma efforts to marketing is an attempt to make these activities more efficient. The undisciplined and creative activities that define marketing offer a rich treasure trove of cost savings when made more disciplined and structured. But what about making these activities more effective and value enhancing? How can Six Sigma grow market share or top-line revenues?

The Modified Six Sigma Argument

On the other side of the battle lines is the argument that Six Sigma should be modified to accommodate the special nature of marketing activities. This is the approach that Six Sigma Marketing (SSM) takes. SSM uses a modified DMAIC approach that provides a fact-based, disciplined approach to growing market share in targeted areas by providing superior value. Its focus on value, products and market share is where it differs from the application of Six Sigma to specific marketing activities.

The first step in the SSM approach is identifying specific products or markets that offer the organization its best options for growth. Six Sigma leaders evaluate products and markets using metrics such as current market share, market growth rate and competitive intensity to assess the best targets for the organization. SSM eschews the notion that a company can be everything to everybody, and instead focuses on key market opportunities. This occurs in the Define stage and differs from the more project-oriented approach that traditional Six Sigma uses.

SSM's DMAIC Approach

In the Measure stage of SSM, the Six Sigma team creates a value model for each of the targeted product or markets. This value model is the voice of the market (VOM) that drives all operational and strategic initiatives undertaken by the organization. The VOM replaces agendas, hunches and strategic guessing as the guiding factor in growing market share. Value has been shown to be the best leading indicator of market share and top-line revenue growth. SSM uses superior value creation and delivery to propel growth within the targeted product or markets.

The value model depicts, in numerical terms, the relative trade-off between the two components of value, quality and price. In most cases, quality is the more important driver of value. Within the model, the team identifies and prioritizes the critical-to-quality factors (CTQs), and ranks the CTQs in terms of their impact on value. This provides a focus that does not exist in most quality improvement efforts. Instead of quality being an abstraction, it is now highly granular and actionable, and it is based on how the market defines quality, not internal sources.

A key element of the value model is that it is holistic in nature and does not focus simply on product features. It includes such value creating and delivery components as product support, service, technical support, warranty and other aspects of the complete buyer experience.

In SSM's Analyze phase, teams use a number of tools, including the competitive value matrix, the customer loyalty matrix and the competitor vulnerability matrix, to guide value delivery. These value tools are designed to facilitate the three elements of market share growth:

1. Acquiring new customers (competitive value matrix and competitor vulnerability matrix)
2. Retaining current customers (customer loyalty matrix)
3. Providing current customers with a reason to upgrade, renew contracts, increase purchase frequency and so on (customer loyalty matrix)

An organization's value is relative to that of its competitors. This is part of the buyers' comparative calculus in assessing where to buy. The buyer is asking a simple question: "Is this brand worth it?" By understanding their organization's competitive value proposition, leaders can make better decisions regarding market share growth.

The improve stage can also be called the Enhancement stage. For value leaders, the focus should be on enhancing value to sustain their leadership position. Extending the gap between the value an organization provides and the value provided by the nearest competitor can lead to best in market status.

Value followers will want to improve those elements of the value creation and delivery system that will close the gap. The principal tool used in this stage is value stream mapping. This process is informed by the value model and the conclusions drawn from the Analyze stage. This is when organizations need to enhance or improve their competitive value proposition in accordance to the directives of the market place.

The Control stage of SSM is where leaders put monitoring systems into place to ensure that their competitive value proposition accomplishes what is intended. This control effort focuses not only on the more strategic value proposition, but also can be set up to monitor specific transactions such as sales, repairs, inquires and other customer experiences. This monitoring process acts as a trip wire, providing information where there are potential people, product of process issues that require intervention.

Transforming Marketing

Six Sigma Marketing is a comprehensive approach to growing market share. It is not a project-by-project approach for reducing the costs of marketing activities, but rather an approach that seeks to enhance marketing's effectiveness and efficiency.

For organizations that have deployed Six Sigma or other quality initiatives, the SSM approach provides a user friendly bridge for moving the quality focus from the manufacturing floor to the marketplace. Those seeking to become best in market must shift their focus from a product orientation to a market orientation, from an internal efficiency focus to an external focus. Best in market companies will be those that can make this transformation and make it soon.

Chapter 8: Applying Six Sigma to Marketing

Marketing professionals want to avoid suppressing creativity with tools and structure. Process-centric work may at first seem slow, routine, and burdensome. Moreover, marketing may think statistical analysis can dampen spontaneity and innovation. But our experience suggests that the opposite is true. The Six Sigma model described in this book plans for innovation and creativity to occur. If implemented correctly, a proven methodology averts rework (caused by mistakes), ensures completeness, and reinforces quality standards. A well-constructed method that requires improvement should plan for innovation and identify the appropriate participants. Moreover, Six Sigma can help tackle the new, the unique, and the difficult.

Few dispute the value of measurement. However, that which is easily measured rarely produces real or optimal value. Real value comes from measuring what others cannot or will not measure. This brings to mind a lesson from history. In 1726, Benjamin Franklin wondered if that warm swath of water he noticed crossing the North Atlantic had anything to do with the longer times it took to sail from England to the U.S. Franklin's cousin, Tim Folger, a whaler, knew that sailing around the current as if it were a mountain was much faster than sailing directly through the current to Philadelphia. In 1769, Franklin sold charts in London on "how to avoid the Gulph Stream" that cut westbound travel time up to 50%.

To this day, Folger's map is surprisingly accurate. These measures gave Folger's whaling business a competitive advantage and higher revenue margins.

The benefit of integrating Six Sigma into your marketing processes includes better information (management by fact) to make better decisions. Using the more robust approach reduces the uncertainty inherent in marketing a creative, dynamic discipline. Go-to-market processes with Six Sigma embedded in them can better sustain growth. One way to maintain growth over time is to focus on "leading" indicators of your desired goal. Leading indicators are factors that precede the occurrence of a desired result. Let's say you are concerned about dealing with a weight-induced disease such as a heart attack or diabetes. You could be reactive by regularly getting on the scale to see how much you weigh. Or you could be proactive by monitoring your caloric intake and burn rate. The latter approach of watching what you eat and how much energy you expend during exercise is harder than simply getting on the scale. The latter approach monitors "leading" indicators critical activities that occur before weight gain. The "lagging" indicator takes a snapshot after the occurrence of an event. Lagging indicators force you into a reactive response if the results fail to meet the target. The act of losing weight may be more difficult than measuring the leading indicators of caloric intake and burn rate. The advice of "pay me now or pay me later" comes to mind.

Business lagging indicators involve measuring defects, failures, and time. Lagging indicators can include functional performance measures such as Unit Manufacturing Cost (UMC), quality measures such as Defects Per Million Opportunities (DPMO), and time-based measures of reliability such as Mean Time Between Failures (MTBF). Lagging indicators for marketing include market share and revenue common performance metrics.

A powerful leading indicator is customer satisfaction before a sales transaction (such as satisfaction with an information meeting or advertising piece). Another leading indicator may be the distribution channel's satisfaction with a product (or samples), whereby the salespeople want to use it themselves. Leading indicators help you anticipate whether you will hit the target. Since leading indicators occur before the desired result, you can be proactive in "correcting" poor performance. Armed with this knowledge, marketing can examine initiatives from a different perspective. To drive and sustain growth, performance and quality metrics need to be proactive rather than reactive. Examples of continuous data include cycle time, profit, mass and rank customer satisfaction scores on a scale of 1 to 10. Continuous variables are more informative and describe a process better than discrete or attribute data. Examples of discrete or attribute data include binary yes/no, pass/fail and counts the number of defects. Leading-indicator data, when established as a continuous variable, requires far fewer data samples to draw conclusions and make a decision as opposed to discrete-failure data.

Recall that a marketing methodology should facilitate the customer-product-financial linkages. This requirement seeks a comprehensive scope of marketing's responsibilities from offering inception, through offering development, to the customer experience. This comprehensive scope encompasses a business's strategic, tactical, and operational aspects. Marketing's role in each of these three business areas can be defined by the work it performs in each. This work can be characterized by a process unique to each. These three processes define how marketing's work links the strategic, tactical, and operational areas in a closed-loop fashion.

Let's examine the process that resides in each area. The Strategic Planning and Portfolio Renewal process defines a business's set of marketplace offerings. This strategic activity is fundamental for an enterprise, because it refreshes its offerings to sustain its existence over time. Multiple functional disciplines may be involved in this process, or the enterprise may limit this work to a small set of corporate officers, depending on the size of the enterprise and the scope of its offerings. This process generally calls for a cross-functional team composed of finance, strategic planning, and marketing, and sometimes research, engineering, sales, service, and customer support. A business with a unique strategic planning department may use it as a surrogate for the other various functional areas. If this is the case, the strategy office typically includes people with various backgrounds (research, finance, and marketing). This process can span a year and should get updated on a regular basis. Portfolio planning and management are the foundation from which to build and grow a business. Our experience tells us that successful businesses have marketing play a key role in the Strategic Planning and Portfolio Renewal process.

There are two ways to win at new products. One is to do the projects right; building in Voice of the Customer, doing the necessary up-front homework, using cross-functional teams. The other way is by doing the right projects namely, astute project selection and portfolio management.

Six Sigma can help improve performance in this area.

The Product and/or Services Commercialization process defines the tactical aspects of a business. This process defines, develops, and readies a business's offering for the marketplace. The industry, market segment, and size/scale/complexity of the offering dictate the number of functional disciplines involved in this process and the amount of time it spans. The time frame ranges from several months to several years. A business usually manages this process by establishing a unique project team to develop a single product or services from the portfolio of opportunities. At a minimum, two types of disciplines are needed; technical functions to drive content and customer-facing functions. The technical experts develop the offering and may include engineering, research, and manufacturing. The customer-facing disciplines represent roles along the value chain that interface with a business's customer or client, such as marketing, sales, services, and customer support. In the Commercialization process, marketing may represent the customer-facing touch points throughout the process and may bring in the other functional areas toward the conclusion of the process in preparation for handoff to ongoing operations.

The Post-Launch Operational Management process unifies the operational aspects of a business across the value chain. This process represents long time frames (often years), depending on the life cycle of a given offering (product or service). The offering and go-to-market strategy dictate the variety of functional disciplines involved across the value chain. Again, marketing may play a representative role, integrating multiple functional areas as it manages the product line (or offering) throughout its life cycle.

Marketing professionals typically view their function as a set of activities or projects rather than a set of processes. It may seem unnatural at first to think about marketing work in terms of a process. However, process thinking provides an easily communicated road map that can describe interactivity with other processes. For example, marketing's tactical Product Commercialization process can cleanly map to the technical community's Product Design and Development process. By creating this linkage, the two functions better understand their interdependency with one another and can speak a common language as the output of one process becomes the input of the other's process.

The book The Innovator's Solution, by C. Christensen and M. Raynor, addresses the importance of process thinking. Similar to a business executive forecasting next quarter's performance, the authors ask the reader to predict the next two numbers in two different sequences. The first sequence of numbers is 3, 5, 7, 11, 13, 17, ___, ___. The second sequence of numbers is 75, 28, 41, 26, 38, 64, ___, ___. Do you know the answers? Without knowing the process that describes the sequence, you can only guess with little or no certainty. The answers for the first sequence are 42 and 6. This sequence was determined by tumbling balls in a drum being selected for an eight-number lottery winning. The answers for the second sequence are 2 and 122. They were determined by the sequence of state and county roads found along a scenic route in northern Michigan, heading toward Wisconsin. Christensen and Raynor point out that "results alone cannot predict future outcomes. The process itself must be understood to predict outcomes." Imagine the increased value that marketing could provide if it could improve its ability to predict the results of its work.

To recap, process thinking is used throughout this book. We explore applying Six Sigma concepts to the work of marketing. Marketing professionals' work environment on a day-to-day basis is not a DMAIC-based workflow structure. Marketing's work breaks down into the fundamental process of three key business arenas.

1. **Strategic area:** The Portfolio Renewal process.

2. **Tactical area:** The Commercialization process (commercializing a specific product and/or service).

3. **Operational area:** The Post-Launch Line Management process (managing the launched portfolio) and its go-to-market resources throughout its life cycle, across the value chain.

The natural flow of marketing work starts with strategic renewal of the offering portfolios, to the tactical work of commercializing new offerings, and finally to the operational work of managing the product and services lines in the post-launch sales, support, and service environment. Marketing professionals frequently overlook the fact that their contributions are part of a process (or a set of related processes). They view their work as part of a program or project. However, marketing work can be repeated. The time frame for repetitiveness may extend over a year or more, but nonetheless, the work is procedural in nature. (The American Society for Quality (ASQ) defines a process as "a set of interrelated work activities characterized by a set of specific inputs and value-added tasks that make up a procedure for a set of specific outputs.") Most marketers would agree that "strategic planning" and "launching a product" meet this "process" definition. The Six Sigma approach embraces a process view to communicate its structure and flow of interrelated tasks. Although it may seem unnatural to marketing professionals, the best way to describe Six Sigma for Growth is through a process lens.

The strategic and tactical areas are internally focused; hence, we refer to them as inbound marketing areas. External data is critical to successful portfolio definition and development, and product commercialization. However, the output of those processes is intended for internal use. These process outputs are not yet ready for external consumption. The outputs that are ready for prime-time market exposure are part of outbound marketing. The operational processes involving post-launch product marketing, sales, services, and support are customer-facing activities. Given the different customers of inbound and outbound marketing, the requirements for each differ. These requirements ultimately define the success (or failure) of the deliverables.

Problems can be prevented in inbound as well as outbound marketing processes. Inbound marketing focuses on strategic product portfolio definition and development, and tactical product commercialization. Inbound marketing can cause problems by under-developing the right data needed to renew product portfolios. The data is needed to define specific new product requirements, thereby directing commercialization activities. And inbound marketing data defines launch plans, which determine downstream operational success. You can design and launch the wrong mix of products and hence miss the growth numbers promised in the business cases that were supposed to support the company's long-term financial targets.

Outbound marketing is focused on customer-facing operations. It encompasses post-launch product line management across the value chain (sales and services, including customer support). Outbound marketing can create problems and waste by failing to develop the right data to make key decisions about managing, adapting, and discontinuing the various elements of the existing product and service lines. Outbound marketing also could fail to get the right information back upstream to the product portfolio renewal teams. They need to renew the portfolio based on real, up-to-date data and lessons learned from customer feedback and the Sales and Marketing experts in the field.

The importance of the comprehensive, closed-loop strategic-tactical-operational scope provided the structural underpinnings used to create the unique Six Sigma methods for marketing. Each of these arenas has a flow of repeatable work; a process context that is quite different from the steps found in the traditional Six Sigma methods. However, the fundamental Six Sigma elements from the classic approaches have been maintained; tool-task linkage, project structure, and result metrics. This new work is made up of specific tasks that are enabled by flexible, designable sets of tools, methods, and best practices. The strategic, tactical, and operational processes within an enterprise align with phases that can be designed to prevent problems to limit the accrual of risk and enable the right kind and amount of data to help make key decisions. The traditional methods help you improve and redesign your processes and get them under control. If the objective is to renew portfolios, commercialize products, or manage product lines, a different approach is required that employs a different set of steps we call phases.

Chapter 9: Unique Six Sigma Marketing Methods

A unique Six Sigma marketing method was created for each of the three areas we discussed in the earlier chapter of this book; strategic, tactical, and operational. The method to guide marketing's strategic work is called "IDEA" Identify, Define, Evaluate and Activate. The approach for tactical work is called "UAPL" Understand, Analyse, Plan and Launch. The method to direct marketing's operational work is called "LMAD" Launch, Manage, Adapt and Discontinue.

The strategic marketing process environment has the following four distinct phases, known as the IDEA process for portfolio renewal and refresh.
1. Identify markets, their segments, and the opportunities they offer.
2. Define portfolio requirements and product portfolio architectural alternatives.
3. Evaluate portfolio alternatives against competitive portfolios by offering.
4. Activate ranked and resourced individual commercialization projects.

The tactical marketing process environment has the following four distinct phases, defined as the UAPL process for specific product and/or service commercialization projects.

1. Understand the market opportunity and specific customer requirements translated into product (or service) requirements.
2. Analyze customer preferences against the value proposition.
3. Plan the linkage between the value chain process details (including Sales and Marketing) to successfully communicate and launch the product (or service) concept as defined in a maturing business case.
4. Launch: Prepare the new product (or service) under a rigorously defined launch control plan.

The operational marketing process environment has the following four distinct phases. This process is called the LMAD process for managing the portfolio of launched products and/or services across the value chain.
1. Launch the offering through its introductory period into the market according to the launch control plan of the prior process.
2. Manage the offering in the steady-state Sales and Marketing processes.
3. Adapt the Sales and Marketing tasks and tools as "noises" require change.
4. Discontinue the offering with discipline to sustain brand loyalty.

Each of these processes features distinct phases in which sets of tasks are completed. Each task can be enabled by one or more tools, methods, or best practices that give high confidence that the marketing team will develop the right data to meet the task requirements for each phase of work. A Gate Review at the end of a phase is commonly used to assess the results and define potential risks. Marketing executives and professionals find phase-gate reviews an important part of risk management and decision-making. In the post-launch environment, gates are replaced by key milestone reviews because you are in an ongoing process arena unlike portfolio renewal or commercialization processes, which have a strictly defined end date.

We have described how Six Sigma works in the context of strategic, tactical, and operational marketing processes. It focuses on integrating marketing process structure, requirements, and deliverables (phases and gates for risk management), project management (for design and control of marketing task cycle time), and balanced sets of marketing tools, methods, and best practices.

Recall that if a marketing process is broken, incapable, or out of control, you should use one of the traditional Six Sigma approaches to improve or redesign it. We assume that the strategic, tactical, and operational marketing processes have been designed to function properly.

Marketing processes and their deliverables must be designed for efficiency, stability, and, most importantly, measurable results; hence the importance of Six Sigma. We will work within the IDEA, UAPL, and LMAD processes, applying their accompanying tool-task sets to create measurable deliverables that fulfil the gate requirements. You may choose to call your process phases by different names; that's fine.

What you do and what you measure are what really matter.

Throughout this book, the word "product" refers to a generic company "offering" and represents a tangible product and a services offering. We discuss technology-based products frequently, because of marketing's interdependency with the technical community. In parallel, R&D, design, and production/services support engineering should use growth and problem-prevention-oriented forms of Six Sigma in their phases and gates processes. The Six Sigma approach serves as a common language between the marketing and technical disciplines. The term "solutions" usually involves both technology and services; thus, "product" and "service" encompass the scope of a given solution. Regardless of the offering, the Six Sigma approach we are outlining is the same and can be applied to either a tangible product or a service offering.

Chapter 10: Marketing Function is Different in a Six Sigma World

Six Sigma is changing the way marketing function in an organization operates today.

Consider the following marketing scenario at a company which manufactures consumer-packaged goods:

During an emergency marketing meeting, the market research division discloses that its Brand X, which has recently lost market share, is rated a poor value by consumers in the targeted market. The challenge from the marketing manager is to identify a solution that will reposition the brand. The assistant manager provides a prototypical marketing solution. First, cut the price of the product. Then, develop an advertising program to convince consumers that the product really does provide the quality and benefits they seek. The new advertising campaign, coupled with the reduced price, will substantially enhance the perceived value of the brand in the marketplace.

Cut price and increase advertising. That was the traditional marketing solution in a world before Six Sigma. So how has Six Sigma changed the way the marketing function operates?

Marketing managers must understand that they have a new set of internal partners for the services they provide. These partners are the Six Sigma Champions and Black Belts responsible for the identification and deployment of Six Sigma projects. Six Sigma projects are directed by the voice of the customer, and the marketing department is the information portal through which customer and market information passes into the organization. So, what type of market information does this new set of internal partners need, and how must that information be provided in order to enhance its utility?

Importance of Strategic Value

Marketing has an important role in providing the strategic focus for the rest of the organization. While it is true that corporate executives provide the direction for overall organizational growth, marketing provides the basis for identifying the competitive arenas. These are the products and markets where the organization will carry out its top-level directives. This functional responsibility is critical because without a strategic focus, any information provided to those responsible for Six Sigma projects will lack sufficient clarity to direct and guide those projects.

Within each of the targeted products and markets, marketing must collect and analyze information in such a way as to clearly identify the key drivers of value and their relative importance and constituent components. This means that the information collected must reflect market as well as customer views, because in many instances Six Sigma initiatives have the dual purpose of attracting new customers while retaining current ones. Analysis of the information must also include the ability to identify the relative impacts of quality and price on customer value perceptions. Absent this analysis, many Six Sigma projects develop an over-reliance on cutting costs and neglect a focus on enhancing the overall quality of products and services. Of course, this also means that both marketing managers and Six Sigma Champions and Black Belts must learn to use the tools of multivariate statistics in order to properly interpret the data.

Understanding the Value of Quality

It is incumbent upon the marketing function to both understand and provide a holistic view of how the market defines the value of quality. This requires expanding the view of how value is created and delivered throughout the entire delivery system of the organization. It is essential to understand that value at the point of production does not necessarily translate into value at the point of consumption. Issues of product support, parts availability, service, warranty and so forth all figure prominently into how customers and markets define and evaluate the value offerings of competing suppliers. Consequently, the value information collected and provided by marketing must identify those factors that are critical to quality (CTQ) throughout the organization's value stream.

The marketing role also should include linking value information from the marketplace to internal processes throughout the organization that create and deliver value. This is the process so critical to the identification of Six Sigma projects, linking the organization's processes (inputs) to competitive performance criteria associated with the CTQs (outputs). The tools used to identify the linkages must allow the organization to set project priorities.

Once Six Sigma projects are under way, an important function in the analysis of information is the development of appropriate tracking metrics to monitor market-perceived changes in value based on changes brought about through Six Sigma projects. Black Belts are expert at the identification and use of appropriate metrics for tracking internal process changes. Marketing should partner with Black Belts to identify and use appropriate metrics to track changes in market perceptions.

The integration of Six Sigma into an organization provides marketing with a unique opportunity and a challenge to change its traditional role within the organization. No longer just a vehicle for corporate communications, nor even just a repository for customer information, the role of marketing can evolve to capture the voice of the market, interpreting that voice in order to identify value-based CTQs, and enabling a partnership with Six Sigma to use that information. Each organization's competitive value proposition is an important asset to actively manage. Six Sigma provides the toolkit for process improvements. It is up to marketing to bring onboard a "voice of the market toolkit" to drive those process improvements toward value enhancements leading to increased market share and profitability.

Chapter 11: Six Sigma Organizational Architecture

Six Sigma is a quality methodology that can produce significant benefit to businesses and organizations. Not much text, however, has been written about the structure needed to successfully implement Six Sigma quality within your business or organization. This chapter will focus on roles and responsibilities, as well as required rewards and recognition for a successful Six Sigma quality program.

Roles and Responsibilities

Quality Leader/Manager (QL/QM): The quality leader's responsibility is to represent the needs of the customer and to improve the operational effectiveness of the organization. The Quality function is typically separated from the manufacturing or transactional processing functions in order to maintain impartiality. The quality manager sits on the CEO/President's staff, and has equal authority to all other direct reports.

Master Black Belt (MBB): Master Black Belts are typically assigned to a specific area or function of a business or organization. It may be a functional area such as human resources or legal, or process specific area such as billing or tube rolling. MBBs work with the owners of the process to ensure that quality objectives and targets are set, plans are determined, progress is tracked, and education is provided. In the best Six Sigma organizations, process owners and MBBs work very closely and share information daily.

Process Owner (PO): Process owners are exactly as the name sounds; they are the responsible individuals for a specific process. For instance, in the legal department there is usually one person in charge maybe the VP of Legal that is the process owner. There may be a chief marketing officer for your business that is the process owner for marketing. Depending on the size of your business and core activities, you may have process owners at lower levels of your organizational structure. If you are a credit card company with processes around billing, accounts receivable, audit, billing fraud, etc., you wouldn't just have the process owner be the chief financial officer, you would want to go much deeper into the organization where the work is being accomplished and you can make a big difference.

Black Belt (BB): Black Belts are the heart and soul of the Six Sigma quality initiative. Their main purpose is to lead quality projects and work full time until they are complete. Black Belts can typically complete four to six projects per year with savings of approximately $230,000 per project. Black Belts also coach Green Belts on their projects, and while coaching may seem innocuous, it can require a significant amount of time and energy.

Green Belt (GB): Green Belts are employees trained in Six Sigma who spend a portion of their time completing projects, but maintain their regular work role and responsibilities. Depending on their workload, they can spend anywhere from 10 percent to 50 percent of their time on their project(s). As your Six Sigma quality program evolves, employees will begin to include the Six Sigma methodology in their daily activities and it will no longer become a percentage of their time it will be the way their work is accomplished 100% of the time.

Chapter 12: Six Sigma and the Voice of Customer

Read any Six Sigma Book, attend any Six Sigma conference or talk to any Black Belt and the message is clear; the voice of the customer is a core value of Six Sigma. When Six Sigma is applied with a strategic perspective, the voice of the customer is indeed the necessary starting point.

Six Sigma and Strategy

An important point about Six Sigma deployments is that it makes no sense to divorce Six Sigma initiatives from the organization's strategy. If becoming the low-cost supplier is the strategy, then it makes sense to focus on those areas of the business where costs are out of line. Here the internal voice of the customer is worth listening to. However, if the organization's strategy is one of value creation and market leadership, then it makes much more sense to provide a way for the ultimate customer to direct the Six Sigma efforts. After all, who knows what value is better than the customer? There is a need for consistency between Six Sigma and organizational strategy. Failure to establish this linkage can mean operationally implementing something that is strategically silly. The question is which customer voice to listen to. Most organizations serve multiple sets of customers. For example, financial service institutions serve segments such as single, newly married and retired. Heavy equipment manufacturers serve miners, farmers and building construction companies. Each segment has a voice and the organization must choose which voice to listen to.

The communication process is somewhat more complicated than simply selecting a segment or two. The voice of the customer will vary depending upon the product line or service. In the financial services institution example, the voice of the customer varies between segments as well as within segments. Newly married customers will voice different needs than retired customers and also may voice different needs for different products such as credit cards or home mortgages. The voice of the customer is product/market specific, and the choice of which products/markets an organization chooses to serve is part of its strategy.

The Product/Market Matrix

To best understand the choices that confront an organization regarding the products/markets served, it is helpful to construct a matrix such as the one shown below.

A Generalized Product/Market Matrix

	Market A	Market B	Market C	Market D	Total
Product Line A					
Product Line B					
Product Line C					
Total					

The matrix aligns the two factors that drive revenue within a profit-seeking organization – customers (markets) and the products and services that they buy. Product lines are groups of products that are similar to each other as defined by the customer. They are, for the most part, substitutable within the same product line but not between product lines. For example, different size tractors can be used to do a job but a manure spreader cannot do what a tractor does. Market segments are groups of like customers with similar needs. If the organization is focused on value, these segments will represent either different value criteria or different weights for the criteria.

Focusing on market segments and product lines is intuitive for most marketers. However, there is an equally compelling argument for focusing on the intersection of market segments and product lines. Both market segments and product lines minimize the variance between segments and product lines respectively. This leaves only the within variance as a source of distortion, thus providing a more focused and clearer understanding of the voice of the customer.

Each cell in the matrix represents a strategic opportunity for the organization. Some opportunities are better than others. The task at hand is to identify which of these products/markets the organization will choose to serve and, in so doing, which will define its Six Sigma initiatives.

Now, Which Customers?

The question of which product/market to choose is answered by identifying specific strategic criteria and then applying an evaluation of these criteria uniformly across all products/markets within the matrix. Typical criteria include:

- Market size
- Market growth rate
- Competitive intensity
- Margins within the product/market
- Market share
- Downstream product/service revenues

First, eliminate all non-viable cells where selling a product or service to a specific segment makes little sense. For example, selling home mortgages to retired customers is probably not a viable opportunity. Next, evaluate the remaining cells in terms of the strategic criteria. The best opportunities are those cells that have the best scores on the various criteria. This may mean that, out of a 4×5 matrix (20 potential opportunities); the best opportunities are found within four or five cells.

Does that mean that the organization will no longer serve the other products/markets? No. But the matrix does indicate areas where the organization will not actively invest and therefore will not expend Six Sigma resources. This is where the alignment of Six Sigma and organizational strategy takes place.

Once the products/markets are chosen, the organization must select which voice of the customer to listen to and which will drive Six Sigma projects.

What Should a Company Listen to?

Conventional Six Sigma practice uses customer satisfaction as the key voice-of-the-customer metric. This metric is problematic on two counts:

1. Satisfaction has little linkage to market performance. More and more organizations are forsaking customer satisfaction as the voice of the customer as they begin to understand that happy customers are not necessarily profitable or loyal customers. In fact, companies such as AT&T and Cadillac learned that while their customer satisfaction scores were increasing, market share was actually decreasing.

2. Satisfaction does not account for the interaction between quality and price. This is an important point because too often organizations think that to increase market share they simply have to reduce price. In reality, they may not have a pricing problem but rather a value problem. Customers are not willing to pay the price that the organization is asking for the quality that they are going to receive. The interplay between quality and price is value, and value has proven to be one of the best predictors of market share.

For strategic applications of Six Sigma, getting the right voice of the customer is critically important. Understanding how Six Sigma initiatives are consistent with strategy is the first step. Knowing which customers will provide the correct voice and what to listen to also is important. Customer value is increasingly the metric of choice. It is being adopted because of its linkages to market performance and its ability to better understand the dynamics of customer behaviour. It is a powerful metric for identifying and directing Six Sigma projects and initiatives.

Chapter 13: Value Matters as a Key Metric for Six Sigma Initiatives

A key measurement of Six Sigma effectiveness is the application of appropriate metrics. An organization's profitability is determined by what it chooses to measure and how it measures it. Most companies need to change what they measure. Many companies use customer satisfaction to measure success. They believe that the metrics of customer satisfaction can lead to the identification of Six Sigma projects, and that the results of those projects should increase customer satisfaction.

But now, some business organizations have come to recognize that measures of customer satisfaction may not be the best metric of business performance. They realize that satisfaction has little to do with the conventional metrics of business performance; such as revenues, market share or profitability.

The reasoning is this:
1. Satisfaction is an emotional response, not the sort of cognitive or evaluative response used by companies in most purchase situations.
2. Satisfaction ignores the interaction among quality, image and price. This is essential for understanding the nature of the buying dynamic.
3. Satisfaction has little, if any, linkage to an organization's performance.

As a result, more companies are beginning to use the more actionable metric of customer value.

Customer Satisfaction and Customer Value

Customer satisfaction frequently involves a comparison of expectations to actual experience. The customer's emotional response is typically captured as individual satisfaction attributes through measurements such as surveys. Customers are asked to rate their satisfaction on individual items such as responsiveness, price, fit and finish, taste, etc. These ratings are then treated independently by reporting satisfaction scores for each attribute. As a result, the items that customers are least satisfied with typically go to the top of the list, and are the issues that receive the most attention.

Attempts to correlate the individual attribute scores with overall satisfaction tend to neglect interactions among the attributes. These interactions create real-life buying situations where tradeoffs occur. For example, a customer may give a low survey satisfaction score to the price of a product, thinking it's too high. Yet, when purchasing the product, the customer is willing to accept the higher price in order to gain greater product quality.

Measuring customer value requires a cognitive calculation of tradeoffs. Determining the value of something requires thinking through and evaluating the benefits received from a product or service relative to its alternatives. Value addresses the question of whether the purchase or interaction was

76

worth the trade-off from the customer's perspective. To answer this question, customers must evaluate the performance of a product on its key quality drivers and then relate that performance to an evaluation of price.

Measuring and understanding market definitions and perceptions of customer value require metrics that are completely different from those used for measuring customer satisfaction. The best quality at the best price is the very essence of what value is all about. Value is a proactive measure where satisfaction is a reactive measure.

Customer value is a better fit with Six Sigma than customer satisfaction metrics for two reasons.

First, the metrics of customer value explicitly recognize the importance of quality to success and lead to identification of specific critical-to-quality (CTQ) characteristics.

Second, perceptions of price competitiveness are highly related to quality, and high levels of quality (low defects) are inversely related to cost. In other words, the more a company improves quality by reducing defects, the lower the cost of producing its product, and the more it will be able to charge for that quality, thereby increasing profit margins.

The Linkage with Performance

Six Sigma initiatives should directly relate to the organization's strategy. Regardless of the strategy market penetration, market development, product development or diversification; a key performance metric is market share and one of the best leading indicators of market share is value. Consequently, customer value is a critical metric that should be driving Six Sigma initiatives.

Likewise, if a company's goal is to increase its ROI (return on investment), ROA (return on assets) or ROS (return on sales) then its ability to differentiate its product or service offerings on the basis of value is essential. A company cannot manage what it does not measure.

Research indicates that satisfaction lacks a consistently demonstrable connection to actual customer behaviour and growth. This finding is borne out by the short shrift investors give to such reports as the American Consumer Satisfaction Index. The index, published quarterly in The Wall Street Journal, reflects the customer satisfaction ratings of some 200 U.S. companies. In general, it is difficult to discern a strong correlation between high customer satisfaction scores and outstanding sales growth.

To illustrate the lack of linkage between customer satisfaction and market share, in the 1980s, customer satisfaction scores for Cadillac and AT&T were soaring while at the same time, their market share was dropping.

Customer value has a strong linkage to loyalty, the willingness of a customer to recommend a company's products or services to another and the willingness of the customer to continue to do business with the company.

One reason for poor linkage between satisfaction and organizational performance is that customer satisfaction typically focuses on the organization's own customers and not the market. How can a metric that does not account for the competitive nature or dynamics inherent in the give-and-take of market share, predict market share? It cannot.

Companies that employ the metrics of customer value are able to identify the precise drivers of quality most important to customers. Value also is a key indicator of market share. The metrics of customer value also reveal how markets perceive the trade-off between the improved quality and current price competitiveness. Customer value has a strong linkage to loyalty. Thus, customer CTQs and customer value are critical metrics for identifying Six Sigma initiatives.

Chapter 14: Applying Six Sigma to Marketing to Grow Revenue

A friend of mine who worked for Motorola from the early 80s until the late mid-90s had an opportunity to be part of the Six Sigma Era. Even though Six Sigma as a measurement standard originated in the 1920s, Motorola is credited with applying the methodologies and coining the term "Six Sigma." The philosophy behind the Six Sigma approach is if you can reduce process variation, you can improve organizational effectiveness and efficiencies. According to General Electric (GE) an early adopter of the program; Six Sigma is a "disciplined methodology of defining, measuring, analyzing, improving and controlling the quality in every one of the company's products, processes and transactions with the ultimate goal of virtually eliminating all defects." Originally used to improve engineering and manufacturing, the Six Sigma approach has expanded to include all aspects of organizational performance, including marketing.

Six Sigma enables companies to improve the marketing's strategic, tactical and operational processes as a way to enhance the top line to drive revenue. By applying Six Sigma to marketing you can develop a lean efficient marketing workflow, identify leading indicators of growth and become proactive about performance improvement. Measurement of performance is one of the five fundamental phases in the Six Sigma methodology. Once you begin measuring marketing performance, you can begin to make modifications and improvements. Six Sigma provides both a methodology for process improvement and a way to prove its value.

Six Sigma has two core methodologies; DMAIC and DMADV; one of the key methodologies associated with Six Sigma is DMAIC. DMAIC is used to improve existing business processes. DMAIC includes five steps; define roles, goals, and deliverables consistent with customer demands and the organization's strategy; measure current performance and processes, and collect relevant data for future comparison and improvement, analyze the relationship and causality factors; improve the process to eliminate defects; and control and correct any variances before they result in defects and thereby improve performance.

The five steps for DMADV include; define the goals of the design activity, measure and identify the critical quality, product/process capabilities, analyze to develop and design alternatives to determine the best design, design the process and verify the design. By using the methodology you can create a data-driven, systematic approach to solving business problems that will have a positive impact on customers.

Let's consider how we can apply the DMAIC process to marketing to grow revenue.

1. Define: The role of marketing is to create predictable streams of revenue growth by enabling the organization to profitably identify and secure new customers, and to keep and grow the value of these customers. Therefore, a key ingredient in this step is for marketing to establish goals and deliverables designed to achieve these three outcomes. To fully realize these three outcomes, the various marketing functions will need to be integrated to create a comprehensive and integrated workflow process. This integrated workflow process will then need to be mapped. Once these three elements are completed, new metrics that tie marketing to the business outcomes must be defined and standardized across the marketing organization for the purpose of providing insight into performance and facilitating strategic decisions.

2. Measure: There is no escaping the fact that to be successful in measurement marketing will need data. Without data, performance cannot be measured and improvements cannot be made. The first step in measuring and improving performance is to determine what data exists, where that data is, what data is needed, and how to obtain the data. Customer purchase activity, marketing program results and conversion rates, actual costs for programs and people, lead quality data and lead cost, win/loss ratios, and defections that occur in the buying process are examples of some of the data that will be needed. Once the metrics are defined, the team should use the data to establish a baseline of past expense and performance.

The metrics should be defined not just in terms of the cost but also in terms of how these investments contributed to the company's ability to achieve its goals and generate profitable revenue. The marketing metrics are contingent upon knowing the business outcomes. It is imperative that the business outcomes be clarified and specified before the marketing metrics are established. Business outcomes for example may be related to the specific number of customers to be acquired and at what cost, the specific rate of customer acquisition, the specific lifetime value of a customer, customer loyalty, and specifically how quickly customers adopt new products. By knowing the business outcomes, marketing knows what objectives it needs to achieve and within what parameters. Marketing can now establish the metrics, the performance targets and processes, and measure its performance. Tying marketing metrics to business outcomes forces marketing to transform from a transactional function to a strategic contributor.

3. Analyze: Simply measuring performance will not make it improve. Performance improvement results from deriving insight through the analysis of the data. By analyzing the data and understanding what it means, marketing can determine the degree of impact it is having on the organization, and redesign processes that will improve performance. Creating a dashboard of key business initiatives can help process the data and make it easier to visualize both the impact and opportunities for improvement. Analysis leads right into the improve step.

4. Improve: A performance-driven organization welcomes opportunities for improvement. The main purpose of applying Six Sigma to marketing is to determine how to improve performance and processes. Data analysis should result in valuable insights that generate possibilities for improvement. These possibilities for improvement can include enhancements in tools, systems, processes, and skills. Even though change is disruptive, developing new ways to approach the market enables the marketing organization to play a more strategic role.

5. Change and Control: Because marketing prides itself on its creativity, it has often sacrificed control. But the time has come for marketing to document its processes and best practices and to apply these consistently in order to optimize marketing execution.

Applying Six Sigma to marketing will increase marketing's ability to deliver on market requirements, improve the efficiency and effectiveness of the marketing planning process, successfully manage marketing operations, provide transparency into marketing processes, and improve the collaboration between marketing and other groups within the business.

Marketing is a process. Six Sigma is an approach for achieving process excellence. It will help you improve the marketing process by providing tools and techniques for identifying what the marketing process is, including suppliers, inputs, process steps, outputs, and customers. Six Sigma helps you understand the need to determine who owns the process and helps the process owner determine how to improve it. It provides a framework for improving all aspects of this process. It does much more as well.

Chapter 15: Lean Six Sigma Marketing and the Sales Process

A common complaint in companies is that sales are unpredictable; not enough or too much but never matching production capacity. Peaks and troughs are uncomfortable bedfellows for fixed capacity production processes, and most businesses, even non manufacturing businesses, operate best with a steady workflow.

Manufacturing has responded in recent years with waves of initiatives which seek to optimise the production process and match supply and demand more precisely. Lean and Six Sigma have been in the forefront with their battery of process optimisation tools such as Kanban, Just-In-Time and Kaizen. Before that it was the quality movement with ISO9000 and TQM, then Re-engineering when only a complete re-think would do, and the Theory of Constraints which can be utilised with any of these initiatives.

In some cited examples the results have been dramatic. Whilst companies can be understandably reluctant to reveal the extent of savings being made some government bodies have gone public. The Royal Navy saved £110 million without reducing front line capability. The US Navy is even more enthusiastic having saved over $500 million on just one programme.

Marketing has been slow to respond. There is no equivalent to Lean and Six Sigma to help optimise the sales process. Demand management models such as used by the budget airlines have filled the gap for products where price is of paramount importance and the product quickly becomes obsolescent but otherwise marketers have been left trailing in the wake of whichever current management philosophy is producing results. Could some of these techniques, and especially Lean and Six Sigma, make a contribution to improving marketing?

Experts argues that there is much to admire and much to learn from these movements. Taiichi Ohno, the father of the Toyota Production System, has come closest to recognising the problem of matching supply and demand by advocating that the scheduling of work should be driven by actual sales and not sales/production targets. This has been a step forward. There is little doubt that converting sales from a variable to a fixed has led to a smoothing out of production, less work-in-progress and a consequent improvement in 'quality' including delivery on time.

It could be argued, however, that this approach has avoided the core problem of how to get demand and supply to move in concert. It also raises the question of how many sales have been lost as a result of an inability to respond to unpredicted and unplanned demand.

Lean and Six Sigma address this problem. Both are process driven initiatives and both start with the customer. Both also seek to optimise the output of the whole system rather than focusing on local optimisation. Marketers will welcome the fact that the initial focus is on identifying customer needs. Lean seeks to reduce operating expenses by eliminating non value added waste; Six Sigma gets variations under control so improving quality and consistency. Most practitioners now see the two philosophies as complementary. Both have a box of tools designed to capture the 'Voice of the Customer'. Any marketer familiar with modern market research techniques will not feel challenged by any of these.

Where Lean/Six Sigma moves the debate forward is that the process of capturing the Voice of the Customer is built into the process of new product development and, ultimately, production. It is integral to it. Such tools as the House of Quality and Quality Function Deployment are a welcome addition to the marketing toolbox effectively taking over where market research leaves off. The former captures customer requirements from a number of sources into a single diagram pray that it never gets into the hands of your competitors! And the latter converts this information into a manufacturing specification. Lean would emphasise that all non value added product features should be eliminated as 'waste'. The latter is the biggest profanity in the Lean dictionary.

The judgement of what is waste and what isn't is based on the willingness of a customer to pay for the feature. Six Sigma would strive to deliver what is left to the standard required by the customer and to a consistent quality. Marketers will welcome such an appreciation of the importance of identifying customer needs in a production environment. So far, so good. Where Lean/Six Sigma thinking has moved the debate forward is in its process approach as applied to the sales process. Six Sigma sees the sales process as a production line. It is a series of steps to a pre-determined goal creating a customer. The 'customer' has to be defined with care. It may, of course, be outside the company the conventional definition or within the company; another department, the company itself, or even another process.

The implication is that there is nothing within Lean/Six Sigma which prevents marketing from using its techniques to optimise the sales process. Start with defining the 'customer' many would argue that it should be production albeit with a broader definition if the company is a service provider capture the Voice of the Customer, define precisely the product specification, and then determine the steps required to achieve the goal.

Old time marketers will see this as just another form of marketing action plan but there is value in integrating marketing and using a common language. If marketing is going to leverage the sales process, it needs a good grasp of what the steps are and how any actions are going to influence those steps toward the desired outcome. Six Sigma would measure each of the steps to death in a way that would frighten most sales reporting systems.

The essence of Six Sigma is statistical process control but the uncertainties inherent in marketing suggest that this could be well watered down in favour of greater use of visual depictions of variations. Most importantly, by taking a holistic or systems approach, a more predictable outcome from the overall process will be achieved. Optimising one element of the process (marketers will feel happier calling it the marketing mix) does not necessarily result in the optimisation of the whole process.

As stated earlier in this book, Six Sigma has two core methodologies; DMAIC and DMADV. DMAIC is used to improve existing business processes, DMADV for totally new situations (re-engineering addresses the same issue). DMAIC consists of five steps: Define, Measure, Analyze, Improve, and Control. If you define your sales process as the process by which you identify customer opportunities, qualify those opportunities, engage with those opportunities, and close those opportunities, Six Sigma offers a more systematic way to understand, plan, manage, and improve this process.

The idea of using Six Sigma to improve the sales process is innovative but it does make sense. A process consists of related and ordered steps to a predetermined goal. Improving sales and marketing by treating them as an assembly line is not a lot different than building an assembly line to manufacture automobiles. Once you understand that without sales there is no need for production, you start to realise that if you applied the same principles to the sales process that are common to production you would end up with a method of managing the complete sales function which would produce far more predictable outcomes.

The terminology used in Six Sigma is not necessarily helpful. Some re-interpretation will be required to adapt it for marketing use. Defects (waste) will need re-defining; a lost customer, a sales lead that is not followed up, a rejected quotation, a mail shot that does not get a response are all examples of waste. But, once you know what a customer is worth to your company, then you also know what it costs if you do not win that customer.

Since it is either your ability to sell or your ability to fulfil that is keeping your company from growing, a good first goal for marketing is to generate enough leverage in the sales process to meet capacity requirements. Everything will flow back from this position.

After mapping the sales process, defining the defects and building the marketing programs to stimulate these processes you will be able to implement the improvements and monitoring controls that will eliminate the waste from your sales process. Continuing improvement will keep the process on track (Kaizen).

Theory of Constraints (TOC)

Another methodology for continuing improvement in a process environment is the Theory of Constraints.

If Six Sigma can seem a little daunting to the smaller company, TOC is much more accessible tool.

According to TOC every process is subject to constraints or bottlenecks and removing these will bring opportunities to increase sales. Imagine the sales process as a pipeline. TOC argues that opening one tap (or bottleneck) more than another will do nothing to increase flow. You need to open the one which most constricts the flow first and then the next and then the next starting from the source. Only by increasing flow through the first bottleneck can overall throughput be increased.

Whilst this may seem common sense many marketing activities are judged in isolation without regard to their ability to increase the throughput of the whole system. Both Lean/Six Sigma and TOC are concerned with the output of the whole system not the efficiency of the individual sub process.

A simple example applied to the sales process demonstrates the basic point that TOC is making. A new advertising campaign may well stimulate enquiries but if they cannot be processed by the sales team there is no overall benefit to the business.

Similarly, introducing a new training course on closing techniques will have little impact when there are insufficient sales leads being generated.

TOC has a methodology for addresses so called bottlenecks the aim being to optimise the complete system rather than one element in isolation. It can be seen as a more user friendly version of DMAIC and as less time consuming and easier to understand without special training.

Marketing has a long history of borrowing concepts from other disciplines and re-inventing them as its own. The good work done in production over the last 30 years could well be the next step in that long tradition. Systematising the marketing function in order to reduce waste, improve efficiency and increase predictability of sales would be welcomed by all. It also has the by-product of presenting the marketing process in a manner which is closer to production thinking and will help the two functions better understand each other.

Chapter 16: Listen to the Voice of the Market

The voice of the market takes the guess work out of defining quality and provides a roadmap for directing enterprise initiatives for achieving best in market quality.

Successful quality initiatives rely on understanding what quality actually means. The meaning of quality resides in the minds of those who judge it and use it to make their purchase decisions; in other words, the market. Divorced from the market, value or quality has no real meaning. Uninformed definitions of value or quality become mere guesses; sometimes right and many times wrong. The voice of the market takes the guess work out of defining quality and provides a roadmap for directing enterprise initiatives for achieving best in market quality.

Critical To Quality (CTQ) Identification Process

Identifying critical to quality characteristics (CTQs) begins first by identifying the product and/or markets the organization is targeting; the better the focus, the clearer the understanding of how that product or market defines quality. Poorly defined products will result in CTQs that are not only "fuzzy" but also less actionable, making it harder to put the information to work.

Once the targets are identified, the organization can convene focus groups of buyers within those targets with the purpose of identifying how buyers define quality and value. These focus groups should be composed not only of the organization's customers, but also customers of its competitors. The output of these focus groups is a set of performance criteria that comprise an overall quality construct.

Once the criteria have been identified, the organization should put them into a questionnaire and field it to current and potential buyers that comprise the targeted product/market. These buyers again should include not only the organization's customers, but also the customers of competitors. Respondents should be asked to rate their supplier's performance on a 10 point scale, where 1 = poor performance and 10 = excellent performance.

These results should then be subjected to a factor analysis to distil the larger set of individual attributes into a smaller set of factors or latent dimensions. These dimensions are named based on the nature of their content and become the CTQ factors. Their prioritization comes from inserting the potential CTQs into a regression model and generating beta weights for each CTQ.

Consider the most important CTQ, customer focus. The first question that arises is, "What is customer focus?" Suppose the team leader assigned you the task of outlining a plan for improving or enhancing "customer focus." Where would you start? The Six Sigma marketing approach provides a detailed blueprint for identifying the people, product and process options for doing so.

Recall that customer focus is a factor, or latent dimension. Accordingly, it is comprised of a set of attributes that define it.

These attributes are:
1. Treating your organization like a valued business partner.
2. Being responsive to your organization's questions and service needs.
3. Being a company that consistently delivers above and beyond expectations.
4. Company reps having a positive attitude.
5. Company reps promptly making changes to your organization's service when you request them.
6. Company reps resolving problems to your satisfaction.
7. After the sale, company reps resolving problems the first time you call.
8. Company reps accurately representing products and services.
9. Company reps providing clear and concise explanations about the bill.
10. Company reps providing timely training on how to use the products and services.
11. After the sale, the ease with which you can reach the right person to solve your organization's communications needs.
12. Being a company that understands the needs of your business.
13. Proactive communication on promotions or new product and service offerings.

14. Provides easy access to products, service and/or accessories at a convenient retail location.

These attributes are lumped into one factor. Based on the nature of the attributes, the team decided to call this CTQ "customer focus." Another team may have called it something else. In this organization, customer focus, because of its overall importance in the value model.

Instead of having to guess what customer focus means, the individual attributes provide a clear and direct approach to people, product and process initiatives for enhancing customer focus.

For example, think of people, products and processes as the x's that drive the Y – performance of the attributes that comprise customer focus. Changing the x's positively changes the Y in a positive direction.

You could begin by examining your training programs to ensure:
1. Reps are responsive to a customer's questions and service needs.
2. Reps can promptly make changes to service requests.
3. Reps can resolve problems the first time a customer calls.
4. Reps are accurately representing products and services.
5. Reps are providing timely training on how to use products and services.
6. Reps have the ability to explain bills in a clear and concise manner.

In addition, you have to examine the processes that support these customer needs. Do the processes exist to allow reps to be responsive to a customer's question and service needs, make changes to service requests, or resolve problems the first time a customer calls? Are the current processes actually inhibiting their reps from providing the requisite level of service? Do they need changing and improving? Mapping these processes led to options for enhancing the organization's customer focus.

From a product standpoint, do you provide business solutions that satisfy the customer's communication needs? Do you have a mechanism for assessing customers' communication needs?

This process is repeated for each of the CTQs identified in the value model. Identifying CTQs in a market-based manner that eliminates guess work and provides a clear path toward improvement and enhancement is a fundamental part of Six Sigma marketing; a fact-based, disciplined approach for growing market share by providing targeted products and/or markets with superior value. Six Sigma marketing provides the customer with a seat at the quality table. After all, they are the ultimate judge of an organization's quality efforts.

Chapter 17: Guidelines for Making Lean Six Sigma Work in Sales

Numerous businesses have had success implementing Lean Six Sigma in sales and achieving the breakthrough benefits that have become commonplace in other organizational functions and processes. The success stories from industry leaders and innovators offer proof that the methodology works, as well as providing some best practice guidelines for implementing Lean Six Sigma in sales.

Selecting the Right Project Focus Area

A common question for organizations considering the extension of Lean Six Sigma into sales is; "What types of projects are best for applying Lean Six Sigma in sales?" Based on experience as well as the best practices of companies such as GE, Johnson & Johnson, Honeywell and others, six types of projects represent fertile ground for early projects

1. Lead generation
2. Sales proposal process
3. Sales forecasting
4. New product launch
5. Sales force efficiency and effectiveness
6. Voice of the customer

The six project areas can be roughly grouped into two categories. Category 1 consists of the first four project areas. These projects focus primarily on the improvement of sub-processes that are related to or supportive of field sales. Companies often find it helpful to start with a Category 1 project for a number of reasons. First, the processes involved in Category 1 projects are relatively easy to identify, visualize and map. In addition, data and metrics on process performance are relatively easy to collect and define. The processes involved are usually repeatable in a fairly consistent manner and finally, solutions and improvements are easier to identify and implement than in Category 2 projects.

Category 1 projects, however, do not directly increased sales; instead, these projects primarily create improvements in the efficiency of internal processes. For example, generating better qualified leads and speeding the flow of proposals to customers will undoubtedly lead to more revenue. Likewise, improved reliability of sales forecasts will impact the availability of products, which will ultimately impact revenue as well. However, the gains from Category 1 projects will not, by themselves, generate the breakthrough results that have become the hallmark of Lean Six Sigma initiatives. It is the Category 2 project areas; "sales force efficiency and effectiveness" and "voice of the customer"; these generate the breakthrough results. These projects are far more complex and challenging in terms of identifying consistent processes, collecting reliable quantitative data, identifying root causes, and finding and implementing solutions. Nevertheless, because Category 2 projects impact the field sales force and selling processes directly, they create solutions and improvements that drive significant and sustainable revenue and margin growth.

Sales Force Efficiency and Effectiveness Projects (SFE&E)

Companies with a sales force that calls on many customers and represent fairly standard products and services are the best candidates for sales force efficiency and effectiveness (SFE&E) projects. These companies are in such industries as pharmaceutical, medical devices and hospital products, financial services, and information technology. Although sales representatives working for these companies all have more or less the same market and customer opportunities in terms of local territories, products to sell, competition, etc., there is typically significant variation in the performance and results of individual representatives. In Six Sigma terminology, a significant amount of process variation exists which, if eliminated, will yield breakthrough improvement in output; in this case revenue growth.

In SFE&E projects, standard Six Sigma tools such as fishbone diagrams and the 5 Whys are used to identify the root causes of variation in performance and results of different sales. Soft (and difficult-to-measure) factors, such as selling behaviours and skills, are frequently more significant root causes than are hard factors such as job experience. Nevertheless, even soft factors can be addressed effectively. For example, best practice selling behaviours and tactics can be identified and replicated across the sales force, and coaching by sales managers can be applied to reinforce best practices and enable the development of best-in-class selling behaviours. Often, simply measuring and communicating publicly the performance of different sales representatives' results in sales growth. This is no doubt due to the competitive nature of salespeople.

Voice of the Customer Projects (VOC)

Voice of the Customer (VOC) projects are most attractive for companies with a concentrated market and customer segment. These companies operate in such industries as aerospace, automotive and household appliances and have a smaller, highly consultative sales force, typically organized around a few key accounts.

VOC projects are targeted on driving customer share or market penetration by first identifying each individual customer's "basic requirements." Basic requirements are those measurable standards of product, service and relationship quality that a supplier must meet in order to remain a supplier to an account. Of course, meeting basic requirements is not enough to ensure continued sales and customer share growth, especially since competitors within the same account are likewise trying to grow customer share. In order to achieve competitive differentiation, companies must learn what really pleases the customer, and finally what it takes to "delight" the customer. Delight, in this case, means pleasing customers beyond the customers' own expectations.

In a typical VOC project, Six Sigma tools are applied to identify basic requirements, what pleases customers and what is likely to delight them. Root causes or opportunities can then be identified that, when addressed, will enable the supplier to not only meet the customer's basic requirements 100 percent of the time, but also will lead to the discovery of delight factors. Implementing improvements and solutions that address delight factors is ultimately what will lead to breakthrough revenue growth.

Some Common Keys to Success

The selection of the best project or projects to implement in order to bring Lean Six Sigma to sales depends on a number of factors, which are different for every company. However it is important to keep in mind a few things that are key to the success of any implementation.

Lean Six Sigma in sales projects must focus on increasing profitability by driving the top line of the business (revenue), more than just driving down expenses As revenues increase, the productivity and cost-to-revenue ratios of the sales force will improve by definition. However, salespeople will avoid, and even resist, anything that they see as an attempt solely to squeeze costs out of the sales force. On the other hand, they will embrace anything that they believe will help them make more sales.

Involving the field sales force directly in projects is essential, but it should not require pulling people out of the field for extended training sessions and project team meetings. Typically, salespeople can work virtually and remain in the field while still participating in a project. Training in the Lean Six Sigma tools and methods can be done on a "just-in-time" basis and teams can be supported by Black Belts, even if the Black Belts have only limited experience in sales.

As is usually the case with organizational change initiatives, keep it simple. Most implementations require use of a handful of key tools; data collection plans, fishbone diagrams, Pareto charts, 5 whys, and a few others which can be easily adapted for the sales environment.

One final thought: Do it now! Keep in mind that while a company is debating whether or not to bring the powerful Lean Six Sigma methodology to its sales staff, competitors may already be using it.

Chapter 18: A Competitive Edge

Organizations can increase market share and revenues by integrating Six Sigma and marketing. Using Six Sigma has proven highly successful in addressing internal issues where the focus is on reducing production defects and costs. One way to take the methodology to the next level is to integrate it with the marketing function. Marketing offers a portal to an organization's external environment; the competitive marketplace where the emphasis is on increasing market share and revenues.

The New Collaboration

Achieving this integration of Six Sigma and marketing requires significant changes in the way both communities those internal to an organization and those business communities as a whole think and interact. "Six Sigma marketers" should go beyond mere defect and cost reduction in marketing processes. They should concentrate on opportunities to use the discipline and methodology of Six Sigma in the organization's value delivery system, encompassing processes that begin with customer contact and order placement.

Given the discipline and structure of Six Sigma, organizations should focus on integrating marketing into Six Sigma, rather than trying to fit Six Sigma into marketing. Six Sigma training should expand its purview to include a focus on increasing market share and top-line revenues. The integration would require new training because the leap from cost cutting to market share growth involves changing mind-sets, as well as learning new measurement and management tools.

The following shifts are fundamental in helping organizations adapt to a more powerful, aggressive and liberated approach to the marketplace.

1. Speed to Customer - Speed to Market

A fundamental precept of Six Sigma is speed, usually expressed in terms of speed to the customer. The premise behind this is that the less time involved in producing a product, the lower the cost. This thinking works within the limited confines of the production facility, but when applied to the greater arena of the marketplace, speed to market should be the metric. The first to market is usually the one best positioned to achieve rapid gains in market share and market dominance.

2. VOC - VOM

Current thinking puts the voice of the customer (VOC) as the principal director of Six Sigma activities. VOC focuses on the organization's customers as the source of information but does not necessarily account for changes in market dynamics that can affect market share. These changes include competitive actions and reactions, new product introductions, new legislation and rules, new technology and new competitors. Gauging changes in market dynamics requires the organization to monitor not only its customers but also its competitors. These dynamics are captured in the voice of the market (VOM).

3. Market Segments - Product/Markets

A market segment is a group of customers who have similar needs or wants. For example, buyers of tractors can be divided into agricultural buyers, part-time farmers and estate owners. These needs and wants are not only specific to different types of customers, but also are impacted by the products and services these customers use. Agricultural tractor buyers want high-horsepower vehicles, while estate owners want small tractors. Each product/market (large tractors/agricultural buyers or small tractors/estate owners) represents a different source of VOM for the organization. Each product/market will have a distinct set of critical-to-quality factors (CTQs) that drive the value equation.

4. 4Ps - 5Ps

Every marketing undergraduate understands the 4Ps; price, product, promotion and place (distribution). To this group should be added a fifth P; process. Much of an organization's value arrives in the marketplace via a set of processes; order delivery, repair, customer support and parts delivery, to name a few. These processes provide a fertile area for value enhancement.

5. Customer Satisfaction - Customer Value

Conventional wisdom dictates that a satisfied customer is a profitable customer. Many organizations are learning, however, that investing in customer satisfaction efforts has not produced increases in market share or revenues. In fact, many organizations are seeing strong customer satisfaction scores in the face of declining market share. The metric that is the best leading indicator of market share is customer value, the interaction of quality and the price that the market is willing to pay for this quality. The greater the sustainable value an organization can create, the greater its share of the market.

6. Internal Customer - End User

There is only one customer; that is the individual who buys and pays for the organization's products or services. Too many organizations focus on internal customers (IT personnel, auditors, accountants, etc.) for advice in process improvement. Organizations must let marketing lead the charge in end-user identification and in understanding how customers define value and how to get this information back to the quality experts within the organization. Marketing can provide a clear line of sight to targeted product/markets and the needs of their buyers.

7. Manufacturing Floor - Marketplace

Unlike the relatively controllable confines of the manufacturing floor, the marketplace is a more seemingly chaotic environment. Marketplace dynamics; changing legislation, new competitors and so on are, for the most part, uncontrollable. To better understand changes in value definitions brought on by new competitors, organizations will have to access new and more powerful training in sampling and multivariate statistics, such as factor analysis, cluster analysis, multiple regression analysis and value modelling.

8. Cost - Revenue

If cost reduction is the prize of conventional Six Sigma, then revenue generation is the holy grail of Six Sigma in marketing. Clearly both efficiency (cost reduction) and effectiveness (revenue generation) are important to the well-being of the organization because they both drive profitability.

9. Customers - Markets

Instead of simply embracing customers, organizations must understand how markets define value and then become the dominant value provider. An organization gains market share by customer acquisition, retention and loyalty (willingness to re-purchase, sign new contracts and upgrade).

10. DMAIC - DMAIC

The traditional DMAIC roadmap remains basically the same in the integration of Six Sigma and marketing, though some components would have to be different. Here is a look at the five phases of DMAIC, focused on marketing:

- Define focuses on defining the market opportunities (product/markets) offering the greatest opportunity for growth and on quantifying the degree of opportunity, such as product/market growth.

- Measure focuses on collecting VOM for the targeted opportunities identified in the Define stage.

- Analyze, a critically important phase, emphasizes identifying how the product/market defines value, complete with the CTQs and a clear understanding of the quality/price relationship. This phase will require the identification and quantification of: 1) the value propositions of the key competitors, 2) the value gaps that exist between the value leader and the organization, and 3) the key people, product and process issues that underlie this value gap.

- Improve involves developing solutions that target the underlying causes of the value gap, with an eye toward strengthening positive gaps where the organization has a value advantage and improving negative gaps where the organization has a value disadvantage.

- Control requires the development of measurement systems to monitor market changes in the organization's value proposition and market share.

A Better Competitor

Integrating Six Sigma into the marketing function may be more possible in organizations in which Six Sigma is strongly embedded. Incorporating this marketing mind-set in the training of new Six Sigma practitioners is a long-term investment, but one that will allow the organization to ramp up its strategic capacity to compete more effectively. Bringing marketers into the Six Sigma fold may help organizations to jump-start the integration process.

Chapter 19: Customer Winback Concept and Six Sigma

Customer winback is becoming a common marketing practice in many businesses. The process is aimed at winning back disgruntled customers and then retaining them. Businesses restore the relationship with old customers through a combination of diligent investigations and follow-up, promotion and targeted improvements specifically addressing customer concerns. Companies willing to make the commitment to customer winback immediately see that it is a process that begs for the adoption of Six Sigma practices and techniques.

What Six Sigma Can Do for Customer Winback

The Six Sigma methodology provides a means for achieving two objectives of customer winback.

1. Identifying correctable problems which, if resolved, will contribute to the positive improvement of how deliverables are delivered to customers.
2. Providing the basis for re-engaging the disgruntled customer to a restored long-term relationship.

A sales department can apply several key practices, selling to former customers has a much higher success rate (20 to 40 percent) than selling to new prospects (5 to 20 percent). Logically, before actively recruiting for new prospects, organizations should explore the option of bringing former customers back into active relationships and transactions.

Investigations are important to find out why customers left the organization. According to Griffin and Lowenstein, there are five basic reasons:
1. **Bought away:** Price-driven reasons (also covers affordability).
2. **Moved away:** Location change.
3. **Pulled away:** Took their business elsewhere.
4. **Intentionally pushed away:** Undesirable member encouraged to withdraw.
5. **Unintentionally pushed away:** Exit because of potentially correctable problems with poor quality or unmet expectations.

Elaborating on the fifth option, additional sub-categories include unhappiness, improper handling of complaints, disapproval of changes and the feeling of being taken for granted. These are areas upon which management can control through diligence and attention to necessary details. By correcting and preventing those events leading to unintentionally pushing away customers, organizations can successfully achieve customer winback.

Customers who left should be evaluated for their past history and their potential for future contributions. Scoring should consider how likely restarting will occur, and how long the restarted relationship will last. The longer the initial relationship, the more likely it will continue after restarting. Those who left more recently also are more likely to restart.

Best Bet Those Unintentionally Pushed Away

The best chance of winning back a customer arises from those who were unintentionally pushed away. More than half of those who left are willing to participate in an exit interview, and a third will reveal how to resume the relationship. Balancing urgency on the one hand and emotion on the other, it is recommended that to get best results customers be approached to answer questions about their leaving 30 to 60 days after they leave. A neutral third-party is often suitable to elicit this information.

Investigations are not meant to embarrass or interrogate, and should be seen as constructive, not punitive. Below are four steps (prepare, assemble, comprehend and employ) for conducting and managing the information obtained from such endeavours.

1. **Prepare:** Determine what the organization knows and what is missing. (Six Sigma covers this within its Define phase.)
2. **Assemble:** Identify unmet requirements, unheard complaints, priorities and areas of importance, and clearer insights. (Six Sigma addresses this portion in its Measure phase.)
3. **Comprehend:** Having collected the information, determine with data models, regression, and statistical significance, areas that call for action and correction. (Six Sigma adds value during the Analyze phase.)
4. **Employ:** Apply the conclusions to correct problems and improve quality and training. Expand support and resources, and establish

recognitions and rewards to encourage member loyalty. (Six Sigma specifically targets this in the Improve and Control phases.)

Six Sigma clarifies the "how" to fully and successfully implement the intentions of customer winback by providing a structured approach to defining the problem, collecting information through designed experiments, measuring and statistically analyzing outcomes and processes for significance, establishing the voice of the customer (VOC) and elements critical to quality (CTQ), and controlling processes and practices that have incorporated the customer needs and wants.

Example of Using Six Sigma to Regain Customers

Using a specific example, a telecommunications company loses customers due to excessive delays in responding to customer requests. An investigation reveals that people do not want to be kept on hold more than five minutes without talking to an actual person who can give them relevant assistance, and they do not want to be diverted or transferred between departments.

Six Sigma measures processes for responding to requests through a single point of contact, and measures the duration of particular requests. Excessive times are charted and noted for further analysis. A routing system is established to reduce idle time and ensure specialists with information and resources pick up on calls. A timer alarms call centre employees to pick up any call left idle for more than four minutes to reassure them and start the process of data collection and customer engagement (and instilling the VOC and CTQ measures into the process). Control measures are instilled through training and monitoring to ensure improvements are entrenched.

Customers who were unintentionally pushed away due to excessive wait times are induced back with a temporary discount, and a financial guarantee giving an extra payment if they are kept waiting.

With respect to incentives, offering a customer winback discount may induce commitment in the short term and provide for a second chance. After the commitment is re-established, the customer could then resume normal fees and charges. Such discounts should be managed carefully, and applied only after determining that the customer has a good track record and will be a long-term supporter of the organization.

Six Sigma can be applied specifically to help companies retain their customers more effectively and with less overall effort and cost than by continually recruiting and releasing customers to and from their ranks. From this perspective, conducting Six Sigma initiatives is not only desirable, it is essential for the preservation and positive evolution of the organization, and should be a required component of organizational excellence and customer-driven marketing.

Chapter 20: Public Relations and Six Sigma

It is as important for Public Relations (PR) agencies or departments to apply rigorous measurement standards and best practices to internal processes and operations as it is to apply them to its public relations campaigns. Six Sigma can help achieve those improvements.

Six Sigma can be used in every business and every department within a company even in places where many executives might not think it can apply, such as public relations.

While PR professionals focus a good deal of time and effort measuring the results of public relations campaigns, they typically spend relatively little time examining internal operations and measurements unless something goes wrong. If an agency stays within its billable hours or a department stays within its line item budget, and objectives are reached, then success is proclaimed and the team moves on to the next project.

But that is a limited view and assumes that the current way of doing things in the organization cannot be improved. Internal measurements, when done correctly, can significantly improve operations and program results. It is just as important in public relations to apply rigorous measurement standards and best practices to internal processes and operations as it is to apply them to campaigns. This is especially important for public relations agencies looking to justify and maximize the time spent on accounts and for company PR departments trying to get the most out of employees without requiring them to work extra hours.

Measuring Activity is Not Enough

For many companies, just measuring campaign activities is not enough for senior management. Reporting that the PR team called 20 reporters, conducted a special event or secured five articles does not meet management's needs. They want to understand what business objectives those activities accomplished. Public relations units need to apply that same measurement rigor to internal operations; going beyond timesheets and making the budget numbers or press release quotas. The objective should be to measure the true impact, not internal activities.

It is relatively easy to measure activity and output. Unfortunately, that does not give a complete or accurate view. If organizations take the extra step of measuring the true impact, they will be surprised at how much more they can accomplish, and how much they can improve processes. There are many different schools of thought about measurement, and none of them provide a complete solution. But for internal processes, a Six Sigma approach offers a good measurement framework.

Six Sigma is a rigorous and disciplined methodology that utilizes data and statistical analysis to measure and improve a company's operational performance, practices and systems. The Six Sigma process, or DMAIC, is simple in its concept – Define, Measure, Analyze, Improve, and Control. In a nutshell, it involves looking at internal processes and finding ways to improve them that will have a direct impact on the bottom line. It is not quality for quality's sake. It is not improving the monthly report, but rather identifying the essential elements of the report that will resonate with the C-level executives and how to do them faster, with fewer errors, so professionals can spend time on other key activities that contribute to the bottom line.

How Six Sigma's Quantitative Measurement Can Help

Many internal areas in public relations are ripe for quantitative measurement, including:

- Reporting
- Media outreach
- Internal meetings
- Employee communications

The following examples show where a Six Sigma quality approach has been applied in two of these areas to improve operations, satisfaction and results.

Reporting: Regular reporting is essential, both for C-level executives and for agency clients. But too often, reporting is done a certain way because that is the standard style or the way it has been done in the past. By breaking down the components of reporting (creating the report, the form, editing it, etc.) and looking at the parts that are actually read, public relations professionals can better understand where their time is spent and how to streamline the process. Then they can quantify how much each step costs and the impact streamlining may have.

By applying the Six Sigma methodology to the reporting process, one agency reduced the size of a report by 45 percent, increased the amount of the report read and saved more than 10 hours each month, which translates into budget that can be assigned elsewhere. When a client or CEO sees those figures, it is hard for them to argue.

Media outreach: Improving media outreach is not about pitching better or making the time for more focus groups, etc. It is about improving the pitching processes. For instance, conventional wisdom may steer you wrong in determining the most effective times to communicate with reporters by phone and email.

A recent project at one public relations agency found that by applying Six Sigma to help determine the best times for media contacts, 18,240 more interactions with reporters can be expected during the course of a year. All without changing the number of phone calls or emails made or the amount of staff time spent. Obviously, the added interactions will help generate more news coverage and thus significantly impact client happiness and retention.

Once Is Not Enough

As a profession, public relations practitioners need to not only justify what they do, but look at how they do it and provide quantitative ways to measure best practices. Measuring internal processes once, or even annually, is not enough. It is essential to look at all recurring activities regularly and find some way to quantify them that will relate to the top and bottom line and help improve overall performance. It is not always easy, and frequently there will be differences of opinion. But having a methodology in place helps structure the discussion.

By creating a framework for measuring internal processes and determining a quantitative figure for making decisions, PR professionals can put themselves in a strong position and give themselves more time to do what they love.

Chapter 21: Putting Six Sigma to Work in Business-to-Business Sales

When the vice president for sales calls a Black Belt in to talk about sales, the natural inclination for the Six Sigma practitioner is to look for the "pain points" and work with a team to define the problem and build a solution. This approach will help transform the sales process, but it may not improve sales results. That is because the starting point for increasing sales and growing the company's business is not the salespeople, it is the customers. In sales, Six Sigma can be used to uncover the best ways to build, maintain and grow relationships with key customers. Great relationships are the key to increasing sales.

Outside-In Thinking: Sales Start with the Customer

When companies invest in sales force effectiveness, they often start with large scale projects like sales automation or customer relationship management (CRM). The time between analyzing the current state, defining requirements and improving the process can be months or even years. Salespeople with daily, weekly, and monthly targets quickly lose interest; they do not see the connection between process maps and winning customers.

One of the biggest challenges is maintaining an external focus. We often lose sight of the customer when we start thinking about processes and goals.

What matters is how customers want to buy and what they want from our salespeople.

Salespeople today need to have strong business acumen and a commitment to the customer that extends beyond closing the deal. That takes a lot more than lunch and a great personality. Salespeople today work with multiple buyers with complex needs. The buying team looks for support in interpreting the massive amount of data that factor into each buying decision. They also expect the sales team to help them achieve their targets for productivity, cost savings and increased customer service.

Six Sigma can provide a framework for improving the quality of relationships between salespeople and customers. Relationship building has:
1. **A starting point:** The introduction.
2. **A mid-point:** Getting to know each other, learning what the client values and delivering that value.
3. **An end point:** The ongoing strong relationship, where the client recognizes and wants the value the salesperson brings to the relationship.

All of a sudden there is a defined process that matters to the sales force; because great relationships win business.

Focus on What Customers Value in the Buying Process

Six Sigma can have a direct impact on sales results if a company is disciplined in keeping the focus on what customers' value in the buying process. This is not about product attributes, customer service or sales support; although data will probably be uncovered that will lead to improvement opportunities in these and other areas. What it is about is the needs of buyers when making a major purchase decision.

Here is how the standard Six Sigma DMAIC roadmap can be used to strengthen the relationships between salespeople and customers.

Define: What Does Sales Expect to Gain?

The challenge in the Define phase is to convince the sales organization that this is a way for them to improve their relationships with key customers and prospects by gathering unique insights into how buying decisions are made.

1. Engage key stakeholders and content experts to work on the project. As the project team is formed, discuss and document the roles each team member will play, time commitments and expected outcomes. Try to build a cross-functional team that includes front-line salespeople and sales managers assigned to key accounts, customer service personnel, sales support and product managers. Eventually, the company may also include external customers on the team.

2. Clearly define the focus of the project. A problem statement that includes the size of the problem, an hypothesis and a scope diagram will help the team to focus on a specific area. The company may decide to

focus its initial project on a particular region or product line. Avoid starting too big.

Measure: A Loyalty Baseline

Gathering data in a way that allows the team to draw conclusions and act on them is critical. Conducting short interviews with buyers and prospects is a good way to understand their critical-to-quality attributes (CTQs) relative to the buying process. This data can be collected fairly quickly but does require up-front planning and expertise in survey design. Many companies use an objective third party to conduct the interviews.

Customer loyalty extends beyond satisfaction, and directly impacts business results. The customer who values the product or service will continue to buy and will promote it to others.

There are three steps for data gathering:

1. Identify a set of customers and then segment them based on recent behaviour. The project team may want to define the universe of customers based on region, revenue size or product preference. Many organizations are able to leverage data from CRM or other sales applications to create four sub-sets of customers:

- **Loyal Customers:** Existing customers who are buying more from the company.
- **Disloyal Customers:** Existing customers who are buying less or have stopped buying.
- **Wins:** New customers.

130

- **Losses:** Prospects that the sales force did not win.

For example, when the credit card division of a global bank developed its customer loyalty baseline, the sample included customers across a range of industries. They also made a point of including several newer customers so they could understand the impact of recent changes in sales strategies and practices.

2. Interview customers. Use non-biased, skilled interviewers to ask representative customers how they make buying decisions. Create an interview guide to walk through the buying process, asking questions about how the client perceives the company's selling efforts. For example:

- What was your first impression of our salesperson? What value did they bring to your purchase process?
- Were the right people from our organization available and helpful to you during your buying process?
- What did our salesperson do that encouraged you to ask us for a proposal?
- What did our salesperson do for you during the product/service delivery phase?
- What could we do differently to make the buying process easier for you?

The project team also may want interviewers to probe for an accurate understanding of the company's value proposition, services offered or other key differentiators of the products and/or services.

3. Interview the sales force. Ask the company's salespeople the same questions. Probe to see how aware the company's sale force is of the wants and needs of customers.

By interviewing a variety of customers, the project team quickly learns what the company's salespeople are doing (or not doing) to build great relationships. By interviewing the sales force, the team learns how much the sales force knows about what the customer values in the selling process.

Analyze: What Do Customers Value?

Analyzing qualitative data is different from reviewing Pareto charts, statistical print-outs and customer survey results. Time should be allowed for the project team to absorb the data and engage in testing different hypotheses. There are three steps in analyzing the data.

1. Identify key themes. Engage a team of salespeople and other stakeholders in reviewing the feedback from the interviews. Make it easier for them to interpret the findings by organizing it around key themes and contrasting the responses from customers to those of salespeople. Be sure to support the key themes with specific examples so the flavour of the comments are retained and the findings resonate with members of the sales team.

2. Cross reference interview findings with sales performance data. It is also helpful to compare the customer and sales interview data with the

profitability data that was used to develop the initial segmentation. This helps in understanding the correlation between what customers say and their buying behaviour.

3. Drill down to the root cause. When the project team has fully analyzed the sales process from the perspective of the customer and found the key improvement opportunities, map the sales process and evaluate how salespeople spend their time. This will help find opportunities to strengthen the company's sales force and support strong relationships.

When we used this process at one of our clients business, the team gathered some compelling data on what customers' value. We learned that the salespeople who incorporated strategic consulting into their sales process had a 100 percent greater closing rate.

Improve: How Should the Company Sell Differently?

Once it has determined how salespeople deliver value to customers, the project team can develop a focused action plan. Common actions include:

- **Changes in pricing strategy:** A uniform pricing strategy may not meet the needs of all customers.
- **More involvement in product delivery:** Salespeople may need to work actively to stay close to the customer once the deal has been closed.

- **Training to improve consulting skills:** Need may be found for training/development of the sales force.
- **Reorganization of the sales function:** Internal barriers need to be removed so that the company can more effectively serve customers.
- **Cross-functional process reengineering:** Customers may be frustrated by the way in which the company integrates sales/credit/distribution, etc.
- **Sales rewards/incentives:** The Company may need to change its sales incentive scheme to promote strong relationships.
- **Revised value proposition:** Customers can recommend fundamental changes in how the company positions and markets its product.
- **Specific actions to support one major customer:** There may be specific issues with one large customer that merit deeper investigation and action planning.

This Client used the Six Sigma framework to increase the amount of time salespeople spend with customers and cut out low-value-added steps. Focusing on the "order to inquiry" component of the sales process, a cross-functional team was convened for an entire week in a Work-Out session to develop detailed recommendations for changes in the sales process. The session helped to get the team focused and drive results in a short time.

Control: Measuring to Sustain Improvements

Improve is the exhilarating phase – changes are implemented and results begin to be seen. To sustain the momentum, there needs to be a process in place to capture and track data on an ongoing basis. You need to track data from lead generation to close. That can mean going beyond the standard sales measures that capture activity but do not necessarily link to revenue growth. A simple dashboard can keep the CTQ's in front of both company leaders and members of the sales force. These key measures should be communicated regularly on a quarterly or monthly basis.

Teaching the Art of Sales

This outside-in approach starts with the premise that great relationships drive growth. It is clearly a back-to-basics approach. Six Sigma is a toolkit and mindset that helps reduce the mysterious art of relationship-building to a set of steps and actions that can be defined, taught, measured and repeated.

Chapter 22: Difficulties of Implementing Six Sigma in Sales and Marketing

The great opportunity for quality in the twenty-first century lies in sales process improvement. Indeed, quality thinking offers a perspective that can help launch sales, marketing, and customer service into a new frontier of systematic, long-term improvement.

Likewise, Six Sigma has come to represent something of a new frontier for many companies wanting to achieve bottom-line benefits through quality improvement. Its success in capturing attention stems from highly visible proponents like GE's Jack Welch, along with its focus on achieving tangible financial results and application to a broad range of situations.

Combining these two realities the opportunity to improve sales and the momentum of Six Sigma would seem to guarantee a wealth of possibilities for successful improvement projects tied to increasing revenue. Through the lens of Six Sigma, the same types of improvement opportunities found in manufacturing can be found in arenas involving more direct person-to-person and customer interchange. Marketing program yields can be improved, sales cycle times can be reduced, and service can produce fewer defects (for example, customer defections).

The range of genuine opportunity makes Six Sigma sound promising for sales and marketing. In spite of the promise, those experienced with the standard approach to Six Sigma often conclude that delivering it as is to an audience of sales and marketing personnel is far too risky. Why?

What Makes Six Sigma for Sales So Difficult?

Four of the most common causes for failure when a Six Sigma program is presented to sales and marketing can be attributed to its inherent production-centric bias. Having remedied some of Six Sigma's own defects when applied to sales, marketing, and service applications, I am convinced that to be most successful, Six Sigma programs in sales and marketing must recognize and avoid these four obstacles and their related implications, without exception.

1. Inappropriate training program design and content. Course material hastily adapted for sales and marketing tends to rely on poorly chosen examples unrelated to real-world problems these groups must wrestle with every day. This makes it difficult to physically see that Six Sigma training offers a sure-fire way to craft and deliver sales and marketing solutions. Sales are too hard to come by to risk on an assurance that, Try it, you will like it. So it should be no surprise that sales and marketing leadership often fails to demonstrate genuine commitment to Six Sigma, right from the start.

2. Inadequate project support after training. Far too many Black Belts and Master Black Belts

138

supporting projects in this arena have little or no hands-on experience in sales and marketing. They cannot provide the practical, knowledgeable assistance that newly trained Six Sigma personnel require, and they cannot create the necessary rapid, smooth transition from the classroom to projects on the job.

3. Cultural barriers. The culture of sales and marketing is to emphasize the strengths of their products and services, not their defects, and to stress making money over cutting expenses. The culture tends to blame people, not processes, when problems occur. The very word quality when applied to such labour-intensive fields is personalized almost immediately. Six Sigma is often perceived as a potential enemy that could be used to draw attention to personal faults on the one hand and create excuses for poor performance on the other.

4. Internal forces reduce interest in customizing the Six Sigma training approach for sales and marketing. Once successful, some movements develop dogmatic by-the-book tendencies that retard constructive evolution, and some companies approach to adapting Six Sigma is no exception. I have often heard a contorted logic used to justify keeping Six Sigma's training approach the same for everybody regardless of the bottom-line results!

The rationalization goes like this; Six Sigma is so important to our success that everybody must learn the same language and methodologies and go through the same program in the same way. We see some red flags, but we have already spent a bundle, so we will stay the course, train and stick to the program we purchased as is. Negative results and feedback are used to perpetuate a belief that sales and marketing are troublemakers (blaming the people), instead of improving the training or being open to more effective innovative approaches that may not even require such extensive classroom training. Chalk it up to politics, lack of experience, lack of budget; the net effect is the same; insufficient tailoring to audience needs, continued frustration, and poor results. With obstacles coming from both Six Sigma training teams and sales and marketing departments, it seems fitting to ask is customizing Six Sigma for sales and marketing worthwhile?

Is Customizing Six Sigma for Sales Worth the Effort?

Let's put the question another way, and the next step is clear to anyone with true business experience who has the authority and responsibility to take action; since when does it make sense to keep doing the same old thing when it doesn't work?

The good news is that the business results show that a custom-tailored approach can be very successful, and that many improvement principles can immediately be extended to sales and marketing applications. Let me share some brief examples of how quality thinking can be applied, including results from my own client applications.

Six Sigma's orientation to the customer offers a chance to update old views of the sales processes into a more tangible framework that allows systematic improvement. The old-world view and treats sales transactions as mysterious and discrete events, with the customer outside of the world of the sales representative. I have actually heard people call what happens magic.

The more systematic view demystifies sales. This view treats income as the output of a tangible system. As such, that system can be subjected to objective analysis using tools common to Six Sigma and other well-grounded disciplines.

In many ways, the customer's buying process is more important to understand as the suppliers selling process. Where Six Sigma's efforts to improve are concerned, customer behaviour is the ultimate focus. The buying process, like the selling process, can be viewed as a sequence of steps.

An offer must be competitive, presenting such clear overall value that it reduces the number of equivalent substitutes the customer chooses to consider and accept. Charting the customer buying process helps remind us of the customer s golden rule. Who has the gold, makes the rules.

It is important to learn the customer's preferences at the points of customer-supplier contact. Quality assurance and improvement efforts must focus on those critical and highly visible intersections.

Concentration on buyer-seller interaction can reveal previously overlooked opportunities for savings and efficiency. The examples that follow show how great the opportunities can be.

The Bottom Line for Sales and Marketing

My hands-on involvement with many successful sales and marketing improvement projects over the last decade has convinced me that, with the proper packaging, many tools within Six Sigma can be adapted to work very well in sales and marketing. The payback when deployed correctly can be substantial, comparable in magnitude to published surrounding production-centric Six Sigma programs.

For example, in one instance, sales in a division of a large financial firm doubled in a one-year period, over a baseline of nearly £100 million. In another case, sales of an industrial firm grew almost 50% in a single year, approaching one-half billion pounds.

The following cases demonstrate particularly well that a disciplined approach can yield improved processes that in turn produce increased revenue and earnings.

An international Computer Network producer initiated a sales training project to counter a strong threat posed by a competitor.

- **Opportunity:** Reduction of competitive threat.
- **Method:** Flow-charting.
- **Discovered:** Gaps in countermeasures.
- **Solution:** Closed gaps, trained, management reporting.

142

- **Results:** Competitor left market entirely.

Hoping to improve customer service, an agricultural products and genetic research organization simultaneously improved productivity.

- **Opportunity:** Sales and service productivity.
- **Method:** Motion/time study and brainstorming.
- **Discovered:** Customers willing to place routine orders independent of salesperson.
- **Solution:** Gave biggest customers on-line access to their internal catalogue.
- **Results:** Millions of dollars in orders immediately began flowing, bypassing representative intervention entirely; eliminated weekend billing fix-it shift; reduced 15 temporary workers.

An electrical designer and supplier for large-scale buildings, airports, stadiums, and offices needed to improve its acceptance by the market.

- **Opportunity:** Some market regions lagging.
- **Method:** Ruled out typical causes (people, regional market differences).
- **Discovered:** Important differences among regions in pricing policy.
- **Solution:** Changed policy.
- **Results:** Sales increased £150 million in a single year.

In the three cases outlined above, viewing revenue as the output of both the selling and buying processes enabled impressive and timely gains. The way these companies reacted to competitors, offered increased customer convenience, and remedied pricing policies in different regions, provides clear examples of benefits that can accrue when one attends to customers buying processes as least as closely as to one's own selling processes.

Custom-tailoring the standard approach to Six Sigma for a sales and marketing audience is essential in order to avoid the pitfalls and garner the rewards. Given the potential financial rewards and the recognized need for continuous improvement in all aspects of business, the effort required to ensure proper execution can pay off handsomely.

Tangible benefits from quality improvement can come in the form of growth and retention of share, as well as cost savings. Many business people in positions of authority are more confident in their ability to cut costs because expense items seem more tangible, hence more controllable, in principle. My First Principle of Sales Process Improvement stands that outmoded idea on its head. The major variables responsible for what a customer buys are tangible or the customer would not be able to experience them in the first place. Sustained growth and market leadership require a system for discovering and capitalizing on these important variables before the competition.

A systematic approach to problem solving and process improvement improves communication and teamwork, as well. Done right, Six Sigma helps sales, marketing, and service departments focus on a common goal, using a shared backbone of improvement tools. Internal articulation of needs is clearer and the rationale for cross-departmental teamwork more apparent to all.

Since the arena of sales, marketing, and customer service still constitutes a budding frontier for quality, early pioneers will enjoy a big head start. Those who harness the power of quality thinking while the field is still young should enjoy competitive advantages for years to come.

Chapter 23: Generating Support for a Sales Quality Initiative

Applying quality principles to sales often produces nothing but resentment and resistance between the sales and quality departments. Examining sales and quality perspectives, this chapter illustrates a technique that might be useful in getting such a seemingly impossible initiative off the ground.

Is quality initiative in sales an impossible dream?

With the right proposition and simple techniques, not only is it possible but it can also be a successful venture. The goal is to achieve performance improvements similar to those achieved in manufacturing and elsewhere using quality-oriented techniques. Unfortunately, these initiatives often produce nothing but resentment and resistance between the sales and quality departments because they essentially speak different languages. Examining sales and quality perspectives, the following discussion illustrates a technique that might be useful in getting such a seemingly impossible initiative off the ground.

Challenges of Sales Organizations

1. Every sales organization is unique. To determine what the challenges to a quality initiative might be, it is necessary to look closely at how the sales organization's performance is judged. What is the language of sales?

2. Is profitability part of the mix, or is performance based strictly on total orders?
3. What are the top three issues the sales executive might raise at a staff meeting that keep him from attaining his goals?
4. What are the components that make up the success of the sales organization?

The Disparity of Languages

Although processes, measurements, and analysis are basics to quality-trained individuals, understanding the "culture" of the sales team may not be. Aside from the standard problems of human nature, such as resistance to change and fear of failure, the sales culture has many special challenges.

1. Sales organizations have traditionally been managed for results, not for process. Change has been slow.
2. Sales executives are usually bright and hard working but by nature may not feel they have time for analytical thinking.
3. Sales involves people and relationships and attracts expressive, amiable, and driver personalities.
4. Sales training doesn't involve measurement and analysis.
5. Selling involves complex cooperation between many departments; communication is key.

Understanding how quality concepts apply in the sales department is no small task, because virtually all of the literature focuses on manufacturing. The effort required to translate the concepts of quality from one world to the other isn't easy, and few people have seen enough of both worlds to do it.

Applying Quality Principles to Sales

Although selling may never achieve the predictability of an automated production machine, it is a place where the rational principles of quality management can make a huge impact. Consider the parallels to the manufacturing environment. In manufacturing, raw materials of certain kinds are sought. People work with the materials (usually via machines) to transform them into a product someone is willing to pay for. When the product is complete, it can be packaged and shipped.

What is the raw material in sales? In sales, the raw material is people in the marketplace. Sales people work with the individuals in the marketplace (leads or inquiries), transforming them from those who may have no intention of buying into those who do. Producing this stream of buyers is the obvious value-creating function of the sales force.

What Value Does Sales Add?

To be effective, sales must add value not only to their company but also to the customer. How can sales people do this? The answer clearly depends on the nature of the specific sales environment (transactional vs. consultative, new account vs. relationship management, etc.). However, the following list should provide some ideas.

1. Sales people instinctively know they must be appealing to prospects through their appearance, personality, and knowledge. They find prospects, are responsive to them, are easy to deal with, and provide answers to prospects' problems.
2. Just as not all raw materials meet specifications, not all prospects are qualified. Time and energy can be saved for prospects and sales people by working on the right kinds of opportunities to meet their needs.
3. Sales people must do their homework to understand the customer's business and industry issues if they are to be valuable to them.
4. Building relationships with the right people, generating a track record of reliability and truthfulness, demonstrating productive insight, and helping prospects build consensus and commit to action are all valuable services to customers.
5. Communicating effectively, learning the customer's addressable problems, positioning value at the right time to the proper individuals, and using language customers understand are critical.
6. Following up to make sure customers achieve the benefits they were expecting is a hall-mark of a professional sales organization.

Similar lists could be made for the other departments. Improving the quality of these activities can increase the yield of business development, often dramatically.

Translating Quality Terms to Sales Talk

Helping the sales department sell better involves understanding the tactical urgencies of prospecting, qualifying, proposing, and closing business. It implies the skills of a sales manager or sales trainer. These may not be common traits among individuals trained in quality.

Aside from that challenge, applying quality principles in any environment requires getting the basics right. In manufacturing, "Lean" principles clean up the work area, clarify responsibilities, and establish order. Gauge reliability and repeatability studies validate measurements. These things must be done to enhance repeatability and reduce the "noise" in the environment. They are prerequisites for any defect reduction initiative.

Because these terms are foreign to the sales environment, basic "Lean" sales principles are needed that can focus and organize sales activities so implementation can be measured and assessed. The value-add of sales must be clarified. The focus must be turned toward process AND results. Also, the organization must be primed for positive change. Establishing this foundation in the sales department may mean challenging the way things are done. Sometimes the magnitude of the change needed is radical. Obviously, most organizations are NOT ready for that, which is the crux of the problem.

Meeting the Challenge of the Sales Department

There are many possible process improvements in sales, from lead generation to various stages of the sales process. However, for a quality-oriented initiative to work, it must meet some demanding criteria. It should be:
1. An approach designed to increase sales.
2. Based on concepts sales understands.
3. Able to generate useful data that suggest potential improvements (to help build the momentum of the quality initiative).

Qualification Improvement Initiative

One possible area to focus on is the input specifications, also known in the sales world as qualification. For example, an electrical utility was attempting to sell a new array of technical services to its customers. They asked for help with closing skills because their close ratio was less than 10%. Sales people were overburdened, chasing as many deals as they could but not making their numbers. Prospects seemed to delay their decisions over and over. They went with engineering firms they already knew. Or deals simply died for no apparent reason.

When asked, "What is the criteria for a qualified prospect?" the answers were all over the map. For example:
1. The customer needed technical services from time to time.
2. They had an engineering problem they couldn't solve.

152

3. There were specifications, but the project wasn't budgeted.
4. A project was designed and going out for construction bids.
5. A project was in process with an engineering firm they already knew.

With so little in common with these "opportunities," it was clear that the sales people had not been told what constituted a qualified opportunity. As a result, they were indiscriminately throwing customer situations into the sales "hopper" and grinding away, hoping a sale would happen. In manufacturing terms, it was as though they were attempting to add value to scrap. Although most sales organizations might not be as lost as this utility, most sales executives would admit that qualification is a critical sales activity and they can't afford to have sales people working overtime to try to get business the organization does not want.

Chapter 24: Using Six Sigma in Marketing Requires Fundamental Changes

The evolution of Six Sigma necessitates a shift in how the method is used in order for it to drive an organization's holistic strategy. Six Sigma promises a path for a firm's long-term success. However, a company cannot really have this Six Sigma journey without the road running through the marketing department. It is through the deployment into marketing that Six Sigma evolves into a strategic process. The synergy between "good marketing" and "good Six Sigma" creates a holistic strategy for a Six Sigma practitioner.

Often, marketing is one of the last functions to which firms apply Six Sigma methods. One of the reasons for this delay has been the difficulty in applying Six Sigma principles to marketing.

Six Sigma has always required some adaptations to fit in new functions. However, with marketing and business development, these changes are more fundamental. The adaptations needed to use the method in marketing, while challenging, ultimately help Six Sigma to become a strategic driver for the organization; a means of function integration and new business development, as well as the global basis of continuous improvement.

Making Four Adaptations

The application of Six Sigma to marketing involves changing the method's basic function. In particular, companies using Six Sigma in marketing must make four key adaptations:
1. Focusing on customer value.
2. Providing a competitive view.
3. Emphasizing communications.
4. Designing in change.

All four of these adaptations enrich the Six Sigma approach; not only in its application to marketing, but also as it is used throughout the organization. In fact, these adaptations make Six Sigma the guiding principle for the growth-oriented firm.

1. Focusing on Customer Value

Customer value has always been the keynote to quality, although it has sometimes been deemphasized in favour of product consistency, exceeding product specifications and cost reduction. These three key objectives of Six Sigma still remain, but the true value of them lies in the underlying enhancement of customer value. The key insight from marketing is the refocus of quality efforts on the needs and desires of existing and potential customers.

Traditionally, when building a quality function deployment (QFD), the "first house of quality" reflects the connection between the marketplace and the business improvement. In the past, practitioners may have thought of the first house of quality in the same way as the other relationships (houses), representing processes and outcomes that form the QFD. However, with marketing, that first house of quality is far more complicated; it relates the total value up and down the supply chain. In the business-to-business environment, this supply chain has linkage running from basic material producers all the way to the ultimate users.

The supply or value chain involves all forms of value-generating functions within the firm and beyond it. Probably the most critical of the value findings is the diversity of customer needs and desires. There is no simple statement of value. Whether the value is computed normatively, based on economics, or measured as a perceived utility, those values are dispersed. The market has multiple sets of values, always providing the basis of opportunity. The Six Sigma deployment must reflect that diversity by building strength and flexibility into the products and services that the firm offers. This opportunity is often captured by the concept of market segments, where each segment represents a group of potential customers with differing values.

2. The Competitive Environment

Differences in market value are evident in the existence of competing products. If all customer values were the same, only a single highest-valued product would be in the marketplace. The existence of competitors indicates those differences.

Six Sigma activities traditionally have been internally focused. Quality in the Six Sigma realm is usually defined by performance compared to specifications, but not typically against market competition. Once an organization enters the marketplace, however, it faces the competitive environment, and quality becomes a competitive element rather than an objective ideal. Customers purchase multiple products and different customers prefer different vendors, even among those vendors that practice Six Sigma. Different competitors appear to be able to each "exceed the expectations" of different customers. Each may be offering quality in a different form, in different levels of performance and in consistency. This is particularly important to understand when new products are introduced.

Competition, however, focuses not only on the product's physical characteristics, but also on both services and image. Branding is a real phenomenon. Quality, in this regard, is a perception as well as a process. The firm's image, in terms of its brand, reflects its "position" that is, its competitive characteristics, including price, brand and product performance. This position is as much a quality issue as is product performance and consistency. The concept of positioning is obtained from marketing. Positioning provides the external metrics for defining quality and performance in the competitive environment. The goal here is to build, improve and maintain competitive advantage. That advantage is then based on Six Sigma principles.

3.   Communicating Quality

Quality is not merely what quality does it is also what people think quality is. That perception is obtained through communications. Without communications, customers do not know what your product is, nor what your quality is. The value of quality comes from not only how it affects the process and the products, but also how it affects the firm and product image. Communication is critical.

Black Belts may have trouble with this concept, but from a marketing perspective, "All truths are perceptions." While this may be an overstatement, the reverse must be accepted, in that without the perception of high quality, quality itself has far less value in the marketplace.

4.   Driving and Enabling Change

With marketing comes a focus on new products and market development. Marketing is the basis by which a firm's business grows, either through organic development based on existing products and markets, or through radically new businesses. Marketing, in this way, is the "change agent" for the firm.

Quality applied to marketing must likewise accept the change environment. While there is nothing within Six Sigma that limits it to achieving small, singular improvements, the methodology tends to favour incremental progress. Six Sigma has generally favoured applications to established processes and, therefore, established products and customers.

Marketing, on the other hand, must favour growth and change. It is the basis for the flourishing of firms, if not their very survival. There is an accepted truism in business that "90 percent of new business comes from existing customers." While that may be the case, in the long run the survival of the firm comes from its new products and markets. That 10 percent of new customers and applications builds quickly and often represents the totality of the earnings of a firm within a few years.

The consequence of the need for change leads Six Sigma into the task of building in quality. That is, organizations need to refocus their Six Sigma efforts onto the inclusion of quality in the design of products and marketing activities, rather than imposing quality on products and services. Quality itself becomes the product, targeted at providing customer value and enhancing outcomes.

Toward a Strategic Six Sigma

The integration of the four principles described here into the Six Sigma process greatly reinforces its strategic role. Not only does Six Sigma continue to provide the improvement environment for practitioners, but it also can lead to the improvement of the entire business. Making these adjustments helps to converge Six Sigma's tools for process improvement with the strategic tools of business development. This combination greatly expands the scope of Six Sigma and the responsibilities of its practitioners.

Chapter 25: Challenges of Deploying Lean Six Sigma in Pharmaceutical Sales and Marketing

"We're different!"

Practitioners often hear these words while attempting to deploy Lean Six Sigma. While the phrase is sometimes viewed as an excuse to avoid change, in the case of the Sales and Marketing function within a pharmaceutical organization, it may hold some validity.

This chapter explores ten reasons why sales and marketing claim to be different in their implementation of Lean Six Sigma. In some instances, the organizations may be correct in their claim, and the deployment might require some flexibility and creativity to be successful. In other areas, they may really be no different than many other organizations. It is important for practitioners to understand what claims of difference are true and which are false so that they can blend traditional and special techniques to make Lean Six Sigma work in Sales and Marketing.

Fact or Fiction?

Following are the top 10 reasons why those deploying Lean Six Sigma in a pharmaceutical sales and marketing organization claim to be different.

1. It's not clear who the customer is. A first step in any Lean Six Sigma implementation is determining who the customer is. Gathering voice of the customer and improving processes are all focused on improving the customer experience with the organization and its products and services. If practitioners don't know who the customer is, they are blocked from the start.

In the pharmaceutical industry, it is clear who the consumer of the product is; the patient. But the healthcare provider (HCP) recommends the product to the patient and then writes the prescription for that product. The pharmacies actually purchase the product from the pharmaceutical (pharma) manufacturers. Then again, it is the insurance companies and other third-party payers who end up paying for the product. So, who is the Customer? Are they all customers? Who should practitioners gather voice of the customer from? Who should they market and sell to? Certainly it is easy to understand why pharma sales and marketing functions claim that they are different.

But this claim is only partially TRUE. For example, the manufacturers of food products market heavily to the public, yet it is the food chains that purchase the product from them. The consumer eats and pays for the product, so it is a little different than the pharmaceutical situation. While the model of a manufacturer trying to directly influence a consumer; even though intervening organizations are the manufacturer's actual customer is quite common, the big difference with pharma is who pays for the product. That additional level of complexity requires

162

improvement activities to have a different focus than the traditional organization.

2. Measuring the impact of Sales and Marketing efforts is challenging. What is the effect of an advertising campaign? For that matter, what is the impact of a sales rep calling on a physician? Measuring this impact is difficult. If there is an impact, there will likely be a time lag between the sales call and the writing of a prescription for a patient. In addition, changes to multiple aspects of the sales and marketing efforts go on simultaneously, which adds to the difficulty of identifying the single factor that actually impacted sales. So this claim is TRUE and highly relevant. But it does not preclude pharma sales and marketing from the use of Lean Six Sigma.

This challenge, however, does focus attention on the need for projects related to the metrics used to drive the business. One specific area of Lean Six Sigma that is pertinent is measurement system analysis. Measurement systems often are bottlenecks to improvement. Fixing and improving the measurement systems have, in some cases, identified that no improvement to the underlying process was necessary; by fixing the measurements, the so-called problem went away. As to the issue of multiple factors changing simultaneously, design of experiments can address this. A good example of the use of design of experiments in marketing was documented to substantially improve the effectiveness of an email campaign in selling products. The metrics are suspect, and many factors under the Sales and Marketing organization's control are changing at the same time. But Lean Six Sigma can address these issues and improve the effectiveness of the organization.

3. The pharmaceutical industry is highly regulated. In the United States, the Food and Drug Administration (FDA) oversees much of the activities of a pharma firm. Similar institutions oversee the pharma industries in other countries. This oversight tends to limit the opportunity for change, and especially affects which products can be sold, as well as the actual manufacturing processes. It also impacts sales and marketing. Limits and controls on the use of promotional items is just one area that demonstrates this impact. These limits make the claim of a valid distinction TRUE. But just as in the case above, this characteristic of the pharma industry does not preclude the changes that Lean Six Sigma can foster.
It does mean that practitioners must take more care to explore and identify which limits are real boundaries, and which are simply perceived to be boundaries, but can be safely ignored. This is similar to the telecommunications industry when it evolved from a monopoly to a competitive environment. One aspect of Lean Six Sigma is change management. This deals with the people-related issues of facilitating change. Thus, Lean Six Sigma offers a methodology to deal with this resistance to change.

4. Sales and marketing is not a process it is all about relationships. Fully documented process maps and flows don't exist in sales and marketing to the same extent as in manufacturing and other organizational

entities. In fact, they might not exist at all. Lean Six Sigma is a fundamental departure from the traditional thinking of marketers because they often view what they do as a series of independent projects, built on relationships they develop with HCPs.

Then again, the most successful sales reps often are the ones who are organized and plan out what they are going to do on every sales call. They plan their days to maximize the value added to the HCP and to optimize their own time. Whether they realize it or not, these reps are using a process; they are doing more than simply showing up, handing out promotional items and being friendly. In addition, by developing a repeatable sales process, they are overcoming inefficiencies, thus leaving more time for creative work which sales and marketing team members thrive on. Therefore, in this case, the claim of "we are different" is FALSE.

5. Gathering voice of the customer (VOC) can be restrictive and expensive. The FDA, along with other government agencies, is making it harder for pharma sales reps to call on HCPs. The FDA also greatly restricts the ability of pharma sales reps to directly market to or make contact with patients. While sales reps and marketing people can still gather VOC feedback and information from HCPs, they often have to pay an honorarium for this information. Sometimes small focus groups of HCP thought leaders are used to gather VOC of macro issues. Then a larger sample of HCPs is used to refine the VOC.

Because of all the restrictions and compliance issues, gathering VOC can be time consuming and costly. Therefore, pharma is indeed different when it comes to gathering VOC; making their claim of difference TRUE. This means sales and marketing teams must use greater efficiency, thought and care in laying out the design of the VOC data collection. Useful information can be gathered from patients, HCPs, payers and pharmacies, but it might require patience and creativity to reduce the time and cost of gathering the VOC.

6. Data is often unavailable and is discrete in nature. A good deal of quantitative data is recorded by the sales rep, including the number of sales calls for the day, or the time spent with the HCP or number of details delivered or whether second and third messages were given. While this data is useful for analysis, the key to understanding the process and improving it lies with the non-quantitative, or discrete, performance data.

This performance data measures how well the activities are performed, not just whether they were performed or not and how people feel or react to sales reps, products, advertising and messages, which is more difficult to capture. But does the need for this data really set sales and marketing teams apart? No, this is FALSE. All organizations need to have a handle on how their people are performing. Just relying on gross sales or share of market numbers is not adequate to improve performance. Similarly, organizations need to identify those variables that impact sales or market share so that they can take improvement actions. Marketing needs to accurately know the impact and effect of their projects and actions and faces the same challenges in collecting this information.

7. Decentralization presents challenges for improvement team efforts. In a plant or office environment, it is relatively easy to have frequent meetings for the team to work through Lean Six Sigma projects. Sales reps are decentralized, and pulling them from their field activities requires great commitment and flexibility. Many sales organizations are faced with a similar problem. They are reluctant to have team members' travel to a central location to participate in improvement activities. The cost of travel coupled with the lost sales opportunities adds considerable expense to improvement team activities. Many organizations face this same situation, so a claim of difference is FALSE.

To combat this challenge, many decentralized sales organizations are using more creative approaches utilizing electronic meeting technology. And when face-to-face meetings are required to work through critical steps of an improvement project, some organizations design these meetings as full-day or multi-day events to minimize overall travel time and expenses.

8. Sales and marketing leadership view Lean Six Sigma as being only for manufacturing If sales and marketing are indeed a series of processes and that all processes contain waste and that the removal of that waste can yield improvements, then it is clear that

167

Lean Six Sigma is indeed applicable to sales and marketing. While many of the more powerful and rigorous statistical methods used in other parts of the organization may not always be appropriate for the sales and marketing function, there are plenty of basic tools, such as value stream mapping, cause and effect matrix, brainstorming, histograms, box plots and run charts, that can suffice for many of the projects that are done in sales and marketing. In situations where there is sufficient amounts of valid data, there is no reason that sales and marketing people can't utilize the more advanced technical tools of both Lean and statistics. Their claim of a difference is FALSE.

9. Many external influences affect sales of prescription drugs. At a macro-economic level, factors such as disease prevalence, ability to pay for the drugs and governmental approval to sell a drug are just some of the issues to be dealt with. At a smaller scale, there are issues around subtle changes to the marketplace, such as no-call limitations, that distinguish the pharmaceutical marketing environment. In addition, there also is the issue that the writing of a prescription does not actually guarantee the sale of product. For example, individuals close to the border may choose to buy their medicine in another country for price reasons. Furthermore, cultural elements can impact sales, or at least the collection of sales data. For example, in Mexico a HCP can write a prescription for an erectile dysfunction drug. The patient, because of some perceived stigma, may get this filled over the counter in a local Pharmacia where the actual sales information cannot be captured by the company.

Many organizations have recalls or "bad press," which are external influences affecting sales. Is this a valid argument that sales and marketing in the pharmaceutical industry is different? No, this is FALSE. These influences do not prevent Lean Six Sigma from effectively identifying opportunities for improvement in sales and marketing efforts. As process-focused thinking spreads through organizations, opportunities to execute activities at a faster pace, with less waste, will naturally surface.

10. There are barriers to entry. The existence of patent protection as a key barrier to entry makes the pharma industry unique; this is TRUE. But these barriers can provide greater impetus to use Lean Six Sigma. One of the key characteristics of Lean is to identify opportunities to execute tasks and activities faster, and with less waste. So, the faster organizations can bring a product to market (including FDA approval), the more time they have to make use of the protection offered by a patent. The faster organizations can evaluate the effectiveness of a marketing campaign, the sooner they will be able to adjust and improve that same campaign. So, while patent protection does make the marketing of drugs unique, it actually makes it imperative that Lean Six Sigma be used to make the most of the protected period of time. Thus, the monopolistic opportunity afforded to sales and marketing in the pharma industry is unique.

Differences Can Be Overcome

Overall, some of the reasons given as to why sales and marketing are different in the pharmaceutical industry are valid. The metrics used to monitor performance definitely need attention. The oversight by the FDA (and others) creates a natural resistance to change that must be overcome. Gathering VOC is difficult, but can be done. And the unique importance of patent protection is real. While all of these characteristics of the business environment create a distinctive situation, they are amenable to the deployment of Lean Six Sigma to improve the speed and effectiveness of the processes and tasks undertaken in the sales and marketing function.

Chapter 26: Six Sigma Apply to Sales and Marketing (Case Study)

A predominantly sales and marketing-driven company shows that not only does Six Sigma apply to sales and marketing, but the benefits are twice as great as one normally experiences in applying Six Sigma to operations processes.

Every sales force has a few outstanding sales representatives, who always deliver on or above target. What is it, in their way of working (process), which makes them so outstanding? If we identify these processes and give them as tools to the rest of the organization, our belief is that we will increase sales force effectiveness. – Senior Vice President, a Fortune 100 Company

A predominantly sales and marketing-driven company, has shown that not only does Six Sigma apply to sales and marketing, but the benefits are twice as great as one normally experiences in applying Six Sigma to operations processes.

These are the typical concerns of a sales director who is confronted with sending his/her best salespeople to Six Sigma training:
1. How to maximize the time spent off-line, i.e., being trained in Six Sigma techniques or working on projects rather than selling?

2. How to work on enough of the overall sales process to have a significant impact rather than divide into sub-processes, e.g., qualifying sales opportunities, that by themselves will not drive increased sales?
3. How to avoid duplication of effort by mass training of sales representatives who are all working with similar processes, i.e., how to leverage and build on the experience of the first successful sales improvement projects?
4. How to get the buy-in of different salespeople, by product line or country, to using the best practice sales processes?
5. How to measure sales force effectiveness?

The over-arching goal was to improve the processes that contribute to more sales per sales representative. The idea was to use Six Sigma to help identify, capture and keep more business with the same or fewer resources.

Scope of the Projects and Selection of Project Leaders

The organizational challenge was how to work on areas of improvement substantial enough to make a meaningful difference and yet not make the projects too complex. By clustering projects around a common theme (e.g., identifying qualified sales opportunities), individuals could work on sub-processes while contributing to a larger improvement (e.g., the overall tendering process). Workshops were conducted with sales executives to scope meaningful projects across the spectrum of sales and marketing processes.

Each project leader had two deliverables: a "to be" process that solved the problem presented to him by his local sponsor and a "best practice" process that could be adopted by others across the region.

The participants were sales and marketing managers responsible operationally for the processes on which they were working. A number of the participants were clearly opinion leaders and respected as high-performers in their respective businesses.

Structure of the Effort and Leveraging Across the Region

In order to create reference projects for the European region as well as processes that could be adopted broadly, regional representation in the project was needed. The approach taken was to combine the formal Six Sigma Green Belt training with small group workshops and individual coaching. This allowed each project leader to present and get input from their regional colleagues while they themselves learned the Six Sigma methodology.

It was recognized from the outset that the biggest benefits to the business would come from leveraging best practices across the region. It was the responsibility of a steering committee to drive that leveraging.

Several elements were critical to capturing "the big dollars," namely process-oriented dashboards reviewed regularly by local managing directors and the e-enablement of sales planning and execution processes.

Broken Myths About Sales and Marketing

The hardest things to learn were those things everyone believed they already knew. The value of a structured, data-driven approach to improving sales force effectiveness is that it challenges assumptions about what drives sales. Some of the insights were:

1. **Sales call planning:** Activities are managed more than objectives; Sales management tools control activity quantity rather than improve the quality of sales calls.

2. **Stakeholder management:** Top-performing sales people target stakeholders who are the most influential, while average performers call on their friends.

3. **Pricing:** There is no correlation between price discounting and volume.

4. **Professional education:** Formalizing selection and follow-up is critical for improvement of revenue generation.

5. **Capital appropriation:** Each country has a different forecasting method, but it is possible to harmonize the forecasting method.

6. **Setting European list and floor price:** No data-driven process has existed for this critical issue in the past.

7. **Tendering:** It is very surprising that 27 percent of all minimum quantities are missed, considering

this minimum is contractual commitment from customers.

8. **Effective selling time:** Out of a 10.4hour working day, sales representatives spent 3.5hours driving and 3.5hours on non-selling activities.

One participant confessed, "I have been selling for seven years, but it wasn't until now that I really understood what effective selling was about."

Lessons Learned

During the course of the initiative, the project leaders went through the normal stages of a Six Sigma project initial scepticism, hope, exasperation, insight and breakthrough. In retrospect the participants highlighted the following lessons learned:

- "Just by looking at our sales processes more closely through the Six Sigma lens, they start to improve."
- "Sales people are interested in the science, not just the art of selling."
- "The lack of standardized processes is a barrier to proliferating know-how across and between businesses."
- "Standardizing the (tendering) process has reduced errors by 20 percent and time by 40 percent."
- "Clear operational definitions of expected outputs, inputs and process steps are vital for a marketing process like product conversion."

- "The fewer the steps and people involved in the (tendering) process, the higher the quality of our analysis."
- "The time spent up-front clearly scoping projects with your Sponsor, pays off later."
- "Jumping to solutions is bad business practice."
- "Do not underestimate the workload involved in the Six Sigma project, but also don't underestimate the value."

The managers started as a very mixed group, different businesses and each with a different understanding of how their individual business worked. Through the experience they learned a common language that allowed them to get to the substance of what each was doing. That was the key to learning from each other and reaching a new level of performance.

Results

Seventeen of the 18 projects launched were successfully completed with a net annual benefit of $8 million. The solutions developed are now being leveraged from the original five countries and two businesses involved to a total of 10 countries and four businesses for an expected annual benefit of $50 million.

In sales and marketing, Six Sigma not only applies but can yield greater financial benefits than in operations, on average $300,000 per project (unleveraged outside respective project scope). Because processes are initially less well-defined, it pays to invest time in carefully scoping the projects with those sponsoring them, i.e., conduct scoping workshops with sponsors before anyone goes to training. Cluster related projects together to get the full desired effect while keeping the individual projects manageable. Enrol senior managers as project leaders. They will see that the "to be processes" get implemented.

Maximize the use of the time sales and marketing people are spending away from customers, structure the training and project work into a series of shorter, more frequent workshops. Accomplish as much of the project work as possible in the workshops. When working across business units and countries, create a very senior level steering committee to help identify and work toward common goals and leveraging of results. Dedicate someone full-time to structuring and managing the initiative.

Keeping 18 opinionated sales and marketing managers aligned is a challenge. Beyond the financial contribution of the projects, the participants improved their skills as managers and change leaders. Adding science to the art of sales can dramatically increase sales effectiveness.

Chapter 27: Conclusion

A 60 percent failure rate suggests that process change requires behaviour change.

Since Jack Welch, the former chief executive officer of GE, popularized Six Sigma in the late 1990s, the business-management methodology has had a profound impact. Yet, amazingly, the majority of all corporate Six Sigma initiatives - 60 percent - fail to yield the desired results.

Amid rising concern regarding these failures, more corporations across multiple industry sectors are now pulling back on their Six Sigma initiatives, realizing that the methodology by itself is not the cure-all for corporate poor health.

At Home Depot, for example, former CEO Robert Nardelli was ousted after his strict focus on Six Sigma negatively affected worker moral and consumer sentiment. In the American Customer Satisfaction Index rankings, the company dropped from a top spot among major retailers to the bottom in 2005. Profitability soared, but the stock price plummeted.

3M also struggled with Six Sigma, though it seemed promising when first implemented under CEO James McNerney, a former GE executive. Profits initially grew approximately 22 percent a year, but then languished. Experts questioned whether McNerney's and Six Sigma's unyielding emphasis on efficiency stifled 3M's creativity and innovation.

These examples show that companies cannot focus on implementing Six Sigma in isolation. But are there ways to supplement the methodology to improve its likelihood of success? Six Sigma is merely a set of process tools that should be only one part of a more holistic process-improvement strategy. Equal attention must be paid to people, innovation, and customer relationships.

We often note a behaviour-change gap within companies that devote significant resources to the Six Sigma philosophies. The experts driving these initiatives tend to be extremely successful at developing technical changes that positively impact company performance. They typically excel in statistical analysis and in addressing specific parts of the process. Much less specific and robust, however, are their efforts regarding the workers upon whom the company depends. With any significant change in internal processes, just the initial talk of the intended change can be unsettling to a workforce comfortable in its current routine. The situation is exacerbated if management fails to communicate the reasons behind the change and fails to demonstrate strong, visible support for it.

Thus, at Six Sigma locations, a sizable gap may exist. While it might be clear what type of change is needed to technically enhance throughput, the success of that effort hinges on whether that behaviour is modified permanently. Process improvements may perfectly achieve their objectives, but the workforce may not be prepared to accept them as part of their daily routines.

Some of the aspects that make Six Sigma powerful may in fact reduce its overall effectiveness. The methodology employs rigorous statistical analysis to identify defect areas, the correction of which produces better quality, lower costs, and increased efficiency. But while Six Sigma may be very effective at controlling processes, elements that are harder to control, such as employee behaviour and innovation/ideation, can hinder long-term success. Implementing the Six Sigma methodology can still be a very successful approach to process improvement. Many companies have seen their product quality improve, their costs decline, and their efficiency levels increase, directly impacting bottom-line profitability. This success, however, often becomes a short-term phenomenon because companies fail to sufficiently recognize the many factors that impact the long-term sustainability of improvements.

A behaviour-focused approach makes change sustainable. It helps workers modify the way they feel and think about their jobs by aligning attitudes and behaviours with the system and process changes, as well as with the overall direction of the company. Further, it keeps us ever-aware that a technically sound change designed by Six Sigma or similar applications could be at risk of failure unless supported by the appropriate behavioural change.

Keep improving!!